Emerging Pathogens at th

Emerging Pathogens at the Poles: Disease and International Trade Law explores the applicability and possible complicating issues of the SPS Protocol to the polar regions in light of emerging pathogeneses and unknown host and environmental susceptibility and resilience.

It examines the current literature on emerging pathogeneses in the Arctic and Antarctic and the relationship pathogeneses have with human development and movement of goods and people in spreading pathogens in the polar regions. Given the endemic nature of the polar environment and the increasing interest in these regions for tourism and industry, this topic is important to address. The major component of the work is on the relevance of the SPS Protocol and the GATT 1994 Article XX(b) exception on human, animal, and plant health as a barrier to trade which is examined in the context of its application to the Arctic and Antarctic. This book is an introduction to the interdisciplinary thinking required, across both science and law, in order to appreciate the significance of global trade barriers in reducing disease transmission and spread.

The spread of pathogens across boundaries has become an important geopolitical issue and the provisions of international trade law may prove decisive in limiting or exacerbating the spread of disease. Academics and students with initial knowledge of the international trade regime, or those with initial studies in health or polar medicine, will find this cross-over a useful introduction to the complications of food, trade, and disease.

Alexandra L. Carleton is a lawyer (BSc LLB LLM) having worked in Sydney, Australia and London, UK, and an independent researcher on matters of law and science as relating to the Arctic and Antarctic. She is a Doctor of Veterinary Medicine (DVM).

Routledge Research in Polar Law

For a full list of titles in this series, visit https://www.routledge.com/law/series/RRPL

Emerging Pathogens at the Poles
Disease and International Trade Law

Alexandra L. Carleton

Routledge
Taylor & Francis Group

LONDON AND NEW YORK

First published 2021
by Routledge
2 Park Square, Milton Park, Abingdon, Oxon OX14 4RN

and by Routledge
52 Vanderbilt Avenue, New York, NY 10017

Routledge is an imprint of the Taylor & Francis Group, an informa business

British Library Cataloguing-in-Publication Data
A catalogue record for this book is available from the British Library

Library of Congress Cataloging-in-Publication Data
A catalog record has been requested for this book

ISBN: 978-0-367-35667-5 (hbk)
ISBN: 978-0-367-69471-5 (pbk)
ISBN: 978-0-367-80834-1 (ebk)

Typeset in Times NR MT Pro by
KnowledgeWorks Global Ltd.

To my mother, for faith that I would find a path combining law and medicine.

To my father, the support of my academic mind and not questioning my direction.

Contents

Preface

Several volumes have been written about the emerging patterns in global disease and how, when disease infiltrates food products, this may affect trade. Despite the writings, this issue has not made policy highlights. However, with the recent outbreaks in virulent and contagious outbreaks, understanding how the science of transmission may affect our global food supplies increases in importance. Writings that span the known science, the evidence of pathogen spread and patterns of transmission and that apply such science to those international codes which govern trade in food products become highly relevant.

As a researcher and writer that has lived in and found a home in the high Arctic, my concern is in understanding how the science of polar regions may inform non-geographically specific international laws, and how these international laws, which continue to cause debate in their application to the polar regions, may consider or run askew of the relevant science.

This is an initial volume. Its coincidental arrival during COVID-19 could not have been planned; the book was already mostly written when COVID-19 began. This may serve to illustrate the point that a left-hand turn is needed as far as polar disease and trade is concerned, particularly if we hope to carry some vestige of our species, tradable products and indigenous livelihood into the half-century.

The main theme of the book is the applicability and possible complicating issues of the SPS Protocol to the polar regions, particularly in light of emerging pathogeneses and unknown host and environmental susceptibility/resilience. The main objective of this book is to discuss the international law of preventing trade in disease, as relevant to the issue of pathogenic spread across boundaries, in the polar regions.

1 Trading in disease at the poles

1.1 International trade and the SPS protocol

The *WTO Agreement on the Application of Sanitary and Phytosanitary Measures* (SPS Agreement, hereafter the Agreement) is the primary international trade agreement which addresses and around which forms the elements of health and disease which prohibits and allows trade in various products. It begins in the preamble with the reaffirmation:

> that no Member should be prevented from adopting or enforcing measures necessary to protect human, animal or plant life or health, subject to the requirement that these measures are not applied in a manner which would constitute a means of arbitrary or unjustifiable discrimination between Members where the same conditions prevail or a disguised restriction on international trade...

This reaffirmation grants at the outset a right of Nations to restrict trade on the basis of protecting human, animal or plant life or health. The Agreement makes the first step in the connection between trade and outside-state species with the potential of causing harm to within-state intra-species life and health. The nexus among international trade, disease, and animals is specifically made clear in terms of the Agreement with the outline of assessment procedures for determination of appropriate SPS measures outlined in Article 5, which notes "prevalence of specific diseases" can be taken into account in assessment of risk (subarticle 2).

Any measure may be taken to be a sanitary or phytosanitary measure where applied "to protect human life or health within the territory of the Member from risks arising from diseases carried by animals, plants or products thereof, or from the entry, establishment or spread of pests" (Annex A, clause 1c). This clause then specifically links animal products and their trade with human health and safety. Animal and plant life and health are also subject to protection "from risks arising from the entry, establishment or spread of pests, diseases, disease-carrying organisms or disease-causing organisms" (Annex A, clause 1a), including the presence of disease-causing organisms in "foods, beverages or feedstuffs" (Annex A, clause 1b). The Agreement does not mention alien or invasive species which is an oversight because of the relevance of translocated diseases. The *Convention on Biological Diversity* entered into force in December 1993 and has alien invasive species listed as a threat to in-situ conservation of biological diversity (Article 8(h)).[1]

Arguably, the legitimacy for the restriction on trade in Arctic and Antarctic trade terms will derive from the first part of the GATT exception in Article XX(b):

> Subject to the requirement that such measures are not applied in a manner which would constitute a means of arbitrary or unjustifiable discrimination between countries where the same conditions prevail...(author's emphasis)

Known as the GATT food safety exception[2] (Kennedy 2000, 82), this article restricts the prohibitions on trade to those which are not arbitrary, or unjustifiably discriminatory. That is, that trading opportunity is offered where like conditions prevail, satisfying the national treatment and most-favoured nation rules (Kennedy 2000, 82).[3]

The same conditions prevailing have the potential to create two particular situations. First, that conditions at the poles are not created elsewhere and, in line with this, there is the question as to how much science will be allowed to influence law in this regard. Geographical and ecological conditions are as much about geomorphology, climate and wind as they are about seasonal tundra, permafrost and other conditions that hitherto have not been given their full weight in international trade law. Second, the conditions that may find some correlation or similarity in polar regions may create a type of exclusion zone, where goods can be traded latitudinally across countries but Southern movement ought to be restricted within country.[4]

Article XX(b) was the original GATT 1994 provision for food safety[5] (Kennedy 2000, 83), and therefore, the only one relevant to possible trade in animal products in Arctic and Antarctic places. It was the provision that gave rise to the more developed requirements for assessment and verification of food product safety of the Agreement (Kennedy 2000, 83).[6] However, as Kennedy says, "[n]o process exists in the SPS Agreement for challenging the adoption of SPS measures that are less protective of human, animal, or plant life and health than international standards" (Kennedy 2000, 87).[7] The SPS Agreement has a relationship with the GATT 1994 accords, the SPS preamble asserting the connection to the pivotal Article XX(b) of the GATT 1994 Agreement; "Desiring therefore to elaborate rules for the application of the provisions of GATT 1994 which relate to the use of sanitary or phytosanitary measures, in particular the provisions of Article XX(b)".

Prior to Article XX(b) and the GATT accords, the provisions for sanitary and phytosanitary measures, as indeed trade in animals and their products, were thought of as part of agricultural negotiations for GATT. The aim was not to protect against disease but rather minimise "the adverse effects that sanitary and phytosanitary regulations and barriers can have on trade in agriculture, taking into account the relevant international agreements".[8]

1.2 Animals and animal products as tradable products

Before beginning on an understanding of the risks posed to the Arctic and Antarctic as far as prevalence of disease and pests or other pathogens are concerned, we first need an understanding that animals and their products (both edible and non-edible products) are 'tradable' under the terms of the Agreement. Specification of animals and their products being tradable does not occur in the Agreement. The Agreement applies to measures which prohibit the international trade of goods and can be justified on the basis of being necessary to protect human, animal or plant life or health. Thus, at the outset, animals and their products must be a tradable product. Any prohibition of their movement in international trade needs to be justifiable under the terms of the SPS Agreement. The basic premise as far as the SPS Agreement is concerned is that presence of pathogens amongst animals that are traded as consumable goods (food, clothing and crafts) increases the potential of the transfer of pathogens within those products.

1.2.1 Commodity versus product, animals as goods

The SPS Agreement makes no reference to commodity or goods in the sense of animal or animal-derived products. However, the terms are mentioned elsewhere in the international codes concerning animal health and welfare. The OIE (World Organisation for Animal Health) lists commodities as including both live animals and the products, genetic material, and pathological materials of animals: the glossary of the Terrestrial Animal Health Code (TAHC) refers to a commodity as "live animals, products of animal origin, animal genetic material, biological products and pathological material".[9] A product here is just one commodity: commodities involve both the live animals and their parts or products. Commodity, however, is not used in the Agreement. Rather "product" is used, no less than 35 times, beginning in Article 4:

> "Members shall accept the sanitary or phytosanitary measures of other Members as equivalent, even if these measures differ from their own or from those used by other Members trading in the same product, if the exporting Member objectively demonstrates to the importing Member that its measures achieve the importing Member's appropriate level of sanitary or phytosanitary protection. For this purpose, reasonable access shall be given, upon request, to the importing Member for inspection, testing and other relevant procedures."

This raises the question whether the Agreement covers the international trade in live or even whole non-live animals. There is also the question of whether this aligns with the understanding of the commercial sector.[10]

Sanitary trade in terrestrial and aquatic animals and their products is the aim of the Animal Health Code (terrestrial and aquatic, respectively). With the 2018 Memorandum, which brought together the aims of the OIE, the World Health Organisation (WHO) and the Food and Agriculture Organisation (FAO), it was agreed that the OIE standards are the reference for global standards in terrestrial and aquatic sanitary standards.[11] These standards are to be used by members of the WTO to derive their own SPS measures. In this way, the OIE serves a function of an aide both in harmonisation efforts and in the provision of those measures internationally by which members can assess their own SPS measures. The *Terrestrial Animal Health Code* and the *Aquatic Animal Health Code* provides standards for harmonising animal health, zoonoses, animal welfare, and food safety. Further, *The Manual of Diagnostic Tests and Vaccines for Terrestrial Animals* and the *Manual of Diagnostic Tests for Aquatic Animals* harmonise the diagnostic testing conducted for identifying pathogens.

Both the OIE and Codex Alimentarius Commission (Codex) have responsibilities for aiding the effort to derive international standards for food safety to foster efforts for harmonisation. It should be questioned as to whether either organisation has the necessary mandate to be able, however, to provide the necessary guidelines for food quality and assurance for the polar region particularly given the original mandates. In 1925, the International Agreement for the Creation at Paris of an International Office for Epizootics, which established the World Organisation for Animal Health, or OIE,[12] was given the "tasks of developing a worldwide livestock reporting system and expediting trade in livestock without increasing livestock disease". Thus part of its original mandate was to track the trade in livestock and increase its speed (Kennedy 2000, 85).[13]

1.3 Hazard analysis and critical control points (HACCP): Trade into and out of the Arctic and Antarctic

Systems for assessing animal health is an area of necessary research. Standardisation across Members for assessing health of animals and animal products – border inspection agencies, quarantine, disinfection at ports of exit and reporting sometimes to National Contact Points – would aid a better understanding and correlation of efforts to control disease. Standardisation of procedures for risk assessment is covered under the SPS Agreement (discussed later), but this is distinct from prescribing actual bodies and protocols for assessing animal health. It may be that this is considered too much an incursion into national jurisdiction, however, this would help equilibrate systems.

1.3.1 Trade into the Arctic and Antarctic

The HACCP standard operating procedures (SOPs) have become a primary way of controlling the export standards (trade-out) of trading nations.[14] One major area for HACCP SOPs are in abattoirs, from where meat is directly exported. In Northern Finland:

> "Approximately 74% of the reindeer are slaughtered in 19 EU-approved reindeer slaughterhouses. Responsible for the meat inspection and hygiene control are veterinarians working under the lead of the Regional State Administrative Agencies of Lapland. For private consumption and direct marketing, approximately 26% are slaughtered by traditional methods in the field (Regional State Administrative Agencies of Lapland). The European food hygiene legislation (Reg. [EC] No. 852/2004 and Reg. [EC] No. 853/2004) also covers the slaughter and processing of reindeer."[15]

Trade into the Arctic and Antarctic requires an understanding of what virulence and host factors may encourage the spread of disease and this may be difficult with unknown anthropogenic effects on microorganisms.[16]

1.3.2   Trade out of the Arctic and Antarctic

Trade out of the Arctic and Antarctic requires understanding of what pathogens already existent may proliferate in different climes. There is emerging evidence of increasing prevalence of microorganisms from polar origin and with it, the transmission, morbidity, and mortality of other species also increase.[17] Emerging pathogeneses in animals and animal products at the poles is now undergoing the beginning of intense interest. There has been a lack of scientific review and study, with scientific reporting sporadic since the 1980s, hence application of any control system based on scientific knowledge runs short of critical control methods from the outset.

Export from Antarctica may be a challenge as far as disease control and application of the SPS Agreement are concerned, given the jurisdictional complications of it remaining under the governance of the Antarctic Treaty System (ATS). The impact of this jurisdictional quandary on the future of the SPS Agreement's application to the Southern continent is unknown.

1.3.3   Trade within the borders

Arctic indigenous trading, for example, reindeer meat and hides, does not come under the international system for risk assessment and disease monitoring. However, the movement of such products in the Arctic may cover large tracts of land. Where the product is diseased, the movement of either the animal or its slaughtered product, essentially moves the disease to different locations, increasing the potential for infection and pathogen translocation, most particularly where climatic conditions in the translocated place are favourable to pathogen proliferation (including, for example, the presence of more host species and warmer temperature). Whilst the movement of indigenous and the trade in livelihood products raises entitlements of right to trade, right to subsistence, right to engage in traditional practices and freedom of movement, where disease spread is concerned, these entitlements may add to the risk. In addition, where the trade in such products brings unregulated and contaminated product into closer contact with borders, it also increases the movement of pathogens across borders.

1.4 Use of Article 6: Measures for endemic areas

The closest the SPS Agreement comes to recognition of endemic areas is under Article 6, entitled "Adaptation to Regional Conditions, Including Pest — or Disease — Free Areas and Areas of Low Pest or Disease Prevalence".

Subarticles 6.1 and 6.2 are specific to exporters that claim pest- or disease-free areas or areas of low prevalence where the onus is on those exporters to prove as such. Although not related to these first two,[18] subarticle 6.3 provides how exporters are to comply. An importer's ability to adapt a measure in question will depend on the exporter's abidance with subarticle 6.3, although may also have recourse to international standards.[19]

Subarticle 6(2) reads:

> "Members shall, in particular, recognize the concepts of pest — or disease-free areas and areas of low pest or disease prevalence. Determination of such areas shall be based on factors such as geography, ecosystems, epidemiological surveillance, and the effectiveness of sanitary or phytosanitary controls."

It almost goes far enough in allowing space for the polar endemism in recognizing that there are disease-free or low prevalence areas which, at least on one reading, may be due to "factors such as geography [or]...ecosystems, [*or the lack of*] epidemiological surveillance, and the effectiveness of sanitary or phytosanitary controls."

However, the necessity for evidence of this may require human testing as part of access requirements for importing Members for inspection, testing and other procedures. Depending on how on-site inspection is carried out, this may nullify the virtue of untouched wilderness being disease-free due to geography and knowledge of pathogen activity. Indeed, as a general comment, the Agreement places no or little emphasis on the ability of or current knowledge of scientific endeavour to understand the disease or pathogen or pest, and thus, determine by deductive reasoning those areas likely to be disease-free or of low prevalence. This, in the author's opinion, is a great oversight of the Agreement. Is there an objective assessment of what is a disease-free area when declared by a nation? If it is up to each importing nation to accept or challenge on the basis of the product whether disease-freedom or low disease prevalence assessment is satisfactory, then does there need to be a general recognition of endemic polar areas as being worth application of special measures due to unique ecosystem factors and with particular regard to a warming climate?

The Agreement does not recognise the need to manage the polar spaces as endemic areas because the conditions of the Article, subarticle 1 are only that Members ensure their SPS measures are adapted to both the area characteristics of the product origin and product destination. Characteristics are taken to mean the "level of prevalence of specific diseases or pests, the existence of eradication or control programmes, and appropriate criteria or guidelines which may be developed by the relevant international organizations" (subarticle 6(1)). In relation to the polar spaces, this is highly questionable as to its efficaciousness. Such areas, with full information absent, can neither have an accurate understanding of the disease or pathogen prevalence, nor have adequate programmes or guidelines. Making a review of adequate SPS measures reliant on the existence of programmes, guidelines or known disease/pathogen prevalence, leaves wide open endemic regions for which these do not exist.

The advocacy during the Uruguay Round for measures to be based on scientific evidence[20] runs afoul because in Arctic and Antarctic communities and uninhabited wilderness, the collection of evidence means intrusion into and possible pathogen transmission into unique and disease-free areas. If anything, the call for scientific evidence ought to have been a sounding call to utilise effectively and continuously, in a dynamic fashion, scientific knowledge about disease and its transmission and containment, including the ability to extrapolate and deduce best practice for safeguarding endemic areas. Yet, it is perhaps not surprising that the text of the Agreement is deficient in this respect. Negotiations to conclude sanitary and phytosanitary measures were not only part of agricultural negotiations, but proved difficult in the Uruguay Round and the text of the Agreement in the end was largely the work of the Director-General Arthur Dunkel.[21] Thus, despite the interconnectedness of yet distinctive aspects addressed by the three subarticles under Article 6, the lack of light shed on the inherent lack of scientific evidence, in particular, relating to wilderness regions does not aid in further understanding the application of the Agreement, in this regard, to the Arctic or Antarctic.

The question then becomes how to apply the Agreement to the Arctic and Antarctic where there is emerging knowledge of disease prevalence and whether a precautionary approach may be used in lieu of full information. More importantly, whether the absence of eradication or control programmes and guidelines, or where such areas are far removed from centres responsible for eradication and control efforts, detrimentally affects the operation of the Agreement in these areas. Finally, whether the interpretation of the SPS within current case law improves the *sui generis* applicability of the Agreement to the Polar space. Aspects of emerging pathogeneses are dealt with in Chapter 2 and the interpretation of the Agreement in Chapter 3.

Notes

1. The Convention on Biological Diversity, 5 June 1992, 1760 U.N.T.S. 69. Under Article 8(h), Contracting Parties shall "Prevent the introduction of, control or eradicate those alien species which threaten ecosystems, habitats or species.
2. Kennedy, K. Resolving International Sanitary and Phytosanitary Disputes in the WTO: Lessons and Future Directions, 55 Food & Drug L.J. 81 (2000), 82.
3. Ibid.
4. It has been shown that vectors of disease are often climatically restricted. In Australia, tick vectors have a very predictable distribution across the Northern hotter part of the country and down the East coast, due to climate, environment and host density: Dehhaghi, M., Kazemi Shariat Panahi, H., Holmes, E.C., Hudson, B.J., Schloeffel, R., Guillemin, G.J., 2019. Human tick-borne diseases in Australia. Frontiers in Cellular and Infection Microbiology 9.
5. Kennedy, supra n 1, 83.
6. Ibid.
7. Ibid., 87.
8. General Agreement on Tariff and Trade (GATT) Punta del Este Declaration, Ministerial Declaration of 20 September 1986.
9. Glossary, Terrestrial Animal Health Code, OIE World Organisation for Animal Health http://www.oie.int/index.php?id=169&L=0&htmfile= glossaire.htm 3 August 2019.
10. Prof. Thomson, G. International trade and marketing of animal commodities and products, 2.
11. OIE, World Organisation for Animal Health, "International Standards", https://www.oie.int/standard-setting/overview/ 30 June 2020.
12. Jan. 17, 1925, 57 L.N.T.S. 135.
13. Kennedy, supra n 1, 85.
14. See for example, International HACCP Alliance, Accreditation Application for HACCP Training Programs, February 2001, Texas, http://www. haccpalliance.org/sub/accreditation.pdf July 2020; HACCP International Certification Food Safety Programme, Australian Government, https:// www.ipaustralia.gov.au/tools-resources/certification-rules/1483322 July 2020.
15. Laaksonen, S., Oksanen, A., Julmi, J., Zweifel, C., Fredriksson-Ahomaa, M., Stephan, R., 2017. Presence of foodborne pathogens, extended-spectrum β-lactamase -producing Enterobacteriaceae, and methicillin-resistant Staphylococcus aureus in slaughtered reindeer in northern Finland and Norway. Acta Veterinaria Scandinavica 59, 2–2.

16. Cavicchioli, R., Ripple, W.J., Timmis, K.N., Azam, F., Bakken, L.R., Baylis, M., Behrenfeld, M.J., Boetius, A., Boyd, P.W., Classen, A.T., Crowther, T.W., Danovaro, R., Foreman, C.M., Huisman, J., Hutchins, D.A., Jansson, J.K., Karl, D.M., Koskella, B., Welch, M.D.B., Martiny, J.B.H., Moran, M.A., Orphan, V.J., Reay, D.S., Remais, J.V., Rich, V.I., Singh, B.K., Stein, L.Y., Stewart, F.J., Sullivan, M.B., van Oppen, M.J.H., Weaver, S.C., Webb, E.A., Webster, N.S., 2019. Scientists' warning to humanity: microorganisms and climate change. Nature Reviews Microbiology 17, 569–586. https://doi.org/10.1038/s41579-019-0222-5.
17. Ibid.; Kleinteich, J., Wood, S. A., Kuepper, F. C., Camacho, A., Quesada, A., Frickey, T., Dietrich, D. R., 2012. Temperature-related changes in polar cyanobacterial mat diversity and toxin production. Nature Climate Change, 2, 356–360. https://doi.org/10.1038/NCLIMATE1418; Paerl, H. W., Huisman, J., 2008. Blooms like it hot. Science 320, 57–58; Huisman J., Codd G.A., Paerl H.W., Ibelings B.W., Verspagen J.M.H., Visser P.M., 2018. Cyanobacterial blooms. Nat Rev Microbiol. 16(8), 471–483. doi:10.1038/s41579-018-0040-1.
18. Panel Report, *India–Agricultural Products*, para. 7.674
19. *US–Animals* para. 7.663
20. Griffin, History of the Development of the SPS Agreement, Module 1. In III. Agreement on the Application of Sanitary and Phytosanitary Measures (SPS) and Agreement on Technical Barriers to Trade (TBT), http://www.fao.org/3/x7354e/X7354e01.htm accessed 10.08.2019.
21. Ibid.

Suggested readings

Cavicchioli, R., Ripple, W.J., Timmis, K.N., Azam, F., Bakken, L.R., Baylis, M., Behrenfeld, M.J., Boetius, A., Boyd, P.W., Classen, A.T., Crowther, T.W., Danovaro, R., Foreman, C.M., Huisman, J., Hutchins, D.A., Jansson, J.K., Karl, D.M., Koskella, B., Welch, M.D.B., Martiny, J.B.H., Moran, M.A., Orphan, V.J., Reay, D.S., Remais, J.V., Rich, V.I., Singh, B.K., Stein, L.Y., Stewart, F.J., Sullivan, M.B., van Oppen, M.J.H., Weaver, S.C., Webb, E.A., Webster, N.S., 2019. Scientists' warning to humanity: Microorganisms and climate change. Nature Reviews Microbiology 17, 569–586. https://doi.org/10.1038/s41579-019-0222-5.

The Convention on Biological Diversity, 5 June 1992, 1760 U.N.T.S. 69.

Dehhaghi, M., Kazemi Shariat Panahi, H., Holmes, E.C., Hudson, B.J., Schloeffel, R., Guillemin, G.J., 2019. Human tick-borne diseases in Australia. Frontiers in Cellular and Infection Microbiology 9.

General Agreement on Tariff and Trade (GATT) Punta del Este Declaration, Ministerial Declaration of 20 September 1986.

Griffin, History of the Development of the SPS Agreement, Module 1. In III - Agreement on the Application of Sanitary and Phytosanitary Measures (SPS) and Agreement on Technical Barriers to Trade (TBT), http://www.fao.org/3/x7354e/X7354e01.htm accessed 10.08.2019.

HACCP International Certification Food Safety Programme, Australian Government, https://www.ipaustralia.gov.au/tools-resources/certification-rules/1483322 July 2020.

Huisman, J., Codd, G.A., Paerl, H.W., Ibelings, B.W., Verspagen, J.M.H., Visser, P.M. 2018. Cyanobacterial blooms. Nature Reviews Microbiology. 16(8), 471–483. doi:10.1038/s41579-018-0040-1.

International HACCP Alliance, Accreditation Application for HACCP Training Programs, February 2001, Texas, http://www.haccpalliance.org/sub/accreditation.pdf July 2020.

Kennedy, K., 2000. Resolving international sanitary and phytosanitary disputes in the WTO: Lessons and future directions, Food & Drug Law Journal 55, 81.

Kleinteich, J., Wood, S.A., Kuepper, F.C., Camacho, A., Quesada, A., Frickey, T., Dietrich, D.R., 2012. Temperature-related changes in polar cyanobacterial mat diversity and toxin production. Nature Climate Change, 2, 356–360. https://doi.org/10.1038/NCLIMATE1418.

Laaksonen, S., Oksanen, A., Julmi, J., Zweifel, C., Fredriksson-Ahomaa, M., Stephan, R., 2017. Presence of foodborne pathogens, extended-spectrum β-lactamase -producing enterobacteriaceae, and methicillin-resistant Staphylococcus aureus in slaughtered reindeer in northern Finland and Norway. Acta Veterinaria Scandinavica 59:2 1–8.

Paerl, H.W., Huisman, J. 2008. Blooms like it hot. Science 320, 57–58.

Terrestrial Animal Health Code, OIE World Organisation for Animal Health http://www.oie.int/index.php?id=169&L=0&htmfile=glossaire.htm 3 August 2019.

2   Emerging pathogeneses at the poles

This chapter will cover the scientific record on the pathogens that are emerging in the Arctic, sub-Arctic, Antarctic and sub-Antarctic regions for the purpose of highlighting both the science and the real questions of containment and host susceptibility. The increasing number of pathogens among wild migratory species, in particular, is a concern, as they transport the pathogens across geopolitical boundaries and into new areas as climate shifts occur. Several of the species discussed (including *Ovibos moschatus* or musk oxen and *Rangifer tarandus* or reindeer) are also a major source of livelihood security for indigenous communities, bringing a new component to uncovering the "common interests of [an]...ever changing [global] community".[1]

The reason that emerging pathogens is important for trade is that traded goods are restricted where disease prevalence affects, in particular, food producing species. Diseases can be zoonotic (transmitted between animals and humans) and pathways to transmitted disease include ingesting of meat products. Where temperatures affect movements of animals, it also affects the movement of bacteria, fungi, viruses and protozoa. Yet, in the cases of the Arctic and Antarctica, the movement of these pathogens is still in its early stages of delineation. Further, there is uncertain knowledge of the bacteria, virus and other pathogens that may either be dormant (non-active and non-sporulating) within the ice or that may be in substratum ice layers too far away for ingestion by animals or humans. With reduced ice cover, the emergence of these unknown pathogens is not known, nor is the effect that they may have on both the animals that roam the lands or that form part of the chain of production for Northern-based communities.

GENETIC PHYLOGENY AT THE POLES

Pathogenic adaptation to a naïve environment comes through several mechanisms:

1 Antigenic variation in a new environment
2 Virulence factors; and
3 Increased host susceptibility

2.1 Emerging pathogeneses of the Arctic

Emerging pathogeneses have been found across the species that are both endemic to the High North and important for livelihood: *Rangifer tarandus* have been found with pestivirus;[2] Musk oxen in Norway with pasteurellosis;[3] Northern seal populations with Phocine Distemper Virus;[4] polar bears on the island of Svalbard with Canine Distemper Virus and Calicivirus;[5] and Arctic Char in the Norwegian sub-Arctic with *Gyrodactylus salaris*.[6] Research shows increasing pathogens in the Arctic region, affecting animals. Pathogens, including *Brucella* spp., *Coxiella burnetti, Chlamydophila* spp.[7] and *Erysipelothrix rhusiopathiae*,[8] have been shown to affect Arctic artiodactyla. The intersecting roles of genetic homogeneity or heterogeneity, the environment, reservoirs, sylvatic carrier populations, and insect vectors are still to be understood in their complexity.[9]

This complex web of interactions affecting the proliferation of emerging disease affects trade in the regions, both trade-in and trade-out. Wild environments can harbour animal species which are carriers of pathogens known to cause disease in domestic animal populations, for example, some pathogens are known to be endemic to *Rangifer tarandus* (reindeer and caribou) which is a circumpolar species,[10] including Cervid herpesvirus 2 (CvHV2),[11] CvHV3 and papillomaviruses 1 and 2 (RtPV1, RtPV2) associated with infectious keratoconjunctivitis (IKC).[12] There is also a hypothesis that *Rangifer tarandus* are carriers of BVDV or pestivirus,[13] which infects domestic livestock with devastating consequences for domestic industry. In this case, the virus found in reindeer is likely to be specific to the species.[14] It has also been suggested that reindeer are a reservoir for Shiga toxin-producing *E. coli*, which is transmissible to humans.[15] In Alaska, North Slope, the muskoxen population "include bovine viral diarrhea, respiratory syncytial virus, *Chlamydophila* spp., *Brucella* spp., *Coxiella burnetii*, and

Leptospira spp."[16] Trade of products both into and out of the higher latitudes poses a higher risk of contamination if lowered resilience and changing climate brings new pathogens which can infect production or food-producing animals. Trade-in may involve products containing pathogens though under export requirements, this ought to be less likely.

2.1.1 Antigenic variation in situ

Antigenic variants evolve in response to environmental stressors and conditions. Genes are lost when unbeneficial and other genes are expressed. Genomic analysis of the pathogens from the Arctic and Antarctic shows that specific adaptation to habitat are encoded in genes and transferred horizontally. A study by Vollmers et al. proves phylogenetic development of gene cluster that code for psychrotrophic ability of the *Octadecabacter* bacteria species. In that study, "*O. antarcticus* constitutes up to 1% of the total bacterial community in the Southern Ocean, and *O. arcticus* up to 23% of the total bacterial community in Arctic sea ice".[17] While only short sequences were shown to be homologous between *Octadecabacter antarcticus* and *O. arcticus*, indicating separate phylogenetics, both do however have specific genes coding for mercury resistance and the formation of gas vesicles which would enable survival in polar environments.[18] Phylogenetic encoding for psychrophilic lifestyle makes translocation unlikely although "cold deep-water currents could be a possible vector for transport of bacteria between both poles".[19]

Flexibility of protein to enable adaptation to the environment has also been found, for example, in *P. halocryophilus* Or1 which has adapted to the Arctic permafrost conditions.[20] Adaptation of *Polaromonas* spp. which inhabit polar glaciers protein genes for: "(i) protection against reactive oxygen species, ultraviolet radiation, and low temperatures; (ii) transport and metabolism of organic compounds; (iii) transport of metal ions; and (iv) resistance to heavy metals".[21] *Polaromonas* spp. are able to adapt to psychrophilic Arctic and Antarctic environments through the use, in particular, of plasmids which carry genes that reduce susceptibility of the host (the bacteria) to the environmental stressors.[22]

Gene sequencing has been demonstrated to have a mutual relationship with the environment and environmental pressures/stressors. However, genetic variance at the poles is still under-researched where the genetic pool has been isolated and functional variants have evolved in relationship with the environment. Similarly, still developing are the effects that warming temperature and competition from new strains of bacteria, virus or other pathogens have on the psychro-trophic survival of these species.

Survival at extreme cold temperatures requires adaptive mecha-nisms, even for pathogens: bacteria known to survive in ice-climates are psychrotrophic (can survive freezing temperatures) and they have genetic coding for oxygen-conserving and mercury tolerance.[23] Cold adaptation is by collection of changes across the genome, includ-ing protein.[24] For example, 39 shock response genes are absent from Arcticibacter.[25] Survival rates change according to growth tempera-ture; cold/heat shock gene presence; salinity tolerance; carbon source utilization; number of monosaccharide metabolism genes; and the heterogenous nature of phylogeny.[26]

2.1.2 Virulence factors

Virulence factors are those that make a pathogen capable of causing dis-ease. Virulence may increase the range of movement across species and ecosystems in known pathogens.[27] Research on virulence specifically affecting change at high latitudes is still in its infancy and is sporadic, but some interesting examples can be found. Expanded Northern ranges have been found for *Setaria tundra*, a parasite nematode found in rein-deer and moose in Northern Finland.[28] While this is due to warming tem-peratures allowing Northern expansion,[29] other parasites have resilience to freezing depending on the host species, for example, *Trichinella nativa* (a parasite) in foxes (clinical study carried out by Davidson et al., 2008).[30]

2.1.3 Animal susceptibility

Animal susceptibility increases when a naïve host is exposed to a pathogen for the first time. Altered host susceptibility increases the risk of transmission of emerging disease.[31] In particular, latitudinal confinement and genetic homogeneity of endemic species lower their resilience and increase their susceptibility to disease. As waters warm, fish species will move North. Boreal fish and fisheries will move into Arctic waters, both introducing new eco-competition and new disease elements.[32] Local endemic species will be subject to by-catch also.[33]

2.1.4 Breaking the Arctic faunal barrier

Various pathogens have been found in naïve species, and in naïve ecosystems, sometimes upon translocation of the vector (the insect or animal capable of playing host to a pathogen without manifesting disease) and sometimes of unknown origin and transmission. *Vibrio parahaemolyticus* was found in Northern sea otters in Alaska of unknown origin.[34] Phocine Distemper Virus (morbillivirus) has been found in gray seal populations in Denmark in areas previously naïve to the pathogen.[35] Polar bear populations have been found with morbillivirus infection[36] and canine distemper virus, a disease of dogs.[37]

A warming climate encourages vectors which prefer hotter and more humid climates to travel further north with the temperatures being favourable to both living and breeding which may result in a shifted arctic faunal barrier, moving further North.[38] This may be seen with fish, a key species of marine health, as predators of plankton and prey to larger marine creatures embarking on poleward shifts.[39] Arctic Ocean Diversity as of August 2019 stated there to be 240 species of fish in the Arctic.[40] As waters warm, fish species shift to higher latitudes, colonizing more Northern latitudes, which in turn may supplant Arctic species through predation, pathogen introduction and Arctic species fragility to these new introductions.[41]

2.2 Emerging pathogens of the Antarctic

Research into the emerging pathogens of the Antarctic is in its infancy, but some research has had interesting findings concerning the increasing prevalence and virulence of pathogens and increasing susceptibility of the endemic environment. Seven novel strains of *Avulavirus,* part of the *Paramyxoviridae* family have been discovered in penguin populations in Antarctica.[42] Even where territorial claims are unsettled or 'frozen', spread of disease by water or aerosol transmission, or even within migration hosts can still occur. Neira et al. reports that Avulavirus was found in Gentoo penguins (*Pygoscelis papua*) and Adélie penguins (*Pygoscelis adeliae*) as part of the epidemiological surveillance of avian influenza in 2014–2016, a highly virulent virus affecting poultry stock globally.[43] The three new species have been named Antarctic penguin virus A (APVA), Antarctic penguin virus B (APVB), and Antarctic penguin virus C (APVC).[44] Four additional species were found and reported last year and named avulavirus 17, 18, 19, and 10-like.[45] Newcastle Disease Virus (NDV), another fatal poultry disease, has also been found in penguins in Antarctica.[46]

2.2.1 Antigenic variation in situ

Clade analysis of *Octadecabacter* spp. shows genetic differences even between those species in the Arctic and those in the Antarctic. Where

Octadecabacter arcticus resides in the polar North, *O. antarcticus* resides in the South. The *Octadecabacter* are bipolar and are phylogenetically linked.[47] Their psychrophilic lifestyle indicates that transmission via a "transit over the warm surface waters of the equator is unlikely"[48] although transmissibility via the colder and deeper water currents could be a possible transport mechanism.[49]

Evolutionary adaptation to polar environments also may have genetic disadvantages for a warming climate. The survival of notothenioids, a dominant suborder of Southern ocean fish[50] historically has depended on its ability to evolve in waters colder and with high oxygen concentration.[51] Part of this response may have been the deletion of a heat-shock response in the Antarctic notothenioids, which occurs in temperate notothenioids.[52] Notothenioids are stenothermal, and have reduced heat shock response which lowers their resilience to change; however they also have duplicate genes[53] contributing to improved fitness where up-regulation is specific to the cold pressures of the Antarctic environment.[54] Icefish have no haemoglobin, losing an oxygen carrier[55] and this "shift from Hb-mediated oxygen transport and delivery to mechanisms based on diffusion may cause higher vulnerability of icefish to warmer temperatures. This feature would be deleterious, if not lethal, in warmer waters."[56] Thus, genetic adaptations can be positive or negative.

Polaromonas spp. are common in high altitude samples collected from air, snow, glacier and ice and have been linked to polar environments, where at least three different high latitude polar locations have been identified as hosting them.[57] The species contains the gene *hipA* leaving a question of survival in a dormant state, enabling localised high latitude survival at the Poles (ibid.). The genus rapidly evolve through horizontal gene transfer enabling adaptation to freezing, thawing, drying, and movement.[58]

2.2.2 Virulence factors

Virulence factors are those by which microorganisms become pathogenic or invasiveness to health. Examining avulavirus in Antarctica, of which seven novel species have been found in the last five years,[59] still has not resulted in understanding its non-pathogenic (non-disease-causing) virulence factors completely. The results are suggestive of penguins being a central reservoir of several species of the avulavirus with some indication of distinct clades in distinct locations, indicating possibly genetic co-evolution with penguin populations, and that the viruses from these reservoirs can infect other avian migratory species.[60] Conversely, virulence factors have been identified from Antarctic samples of *E. Coli* relating to pathogenic capacity in the alimentary tract (called enteropathogenic *E. coli* or EPEC).[61] One virulence factor known as the 'eae gene isolate' which is enteropathogenic has been specifically identified. Yet how and when this virulence factors became part of the commensal microbiota of marine mammals is not yet known, but may involve possible geographic movement or association with human waste, as *E. Coli* is a human commensal, either from other human inhabited places or from human presence in Antarctica.[62]

2.2.3 Animal susceptibility

Animals can be susceptible in a number of ways. Either their naïve status increases the risk of clinical disease manifesting once a pathogen has been infective, or the animal can demonstrate some modification or acclimation, but with immunocompromise, allowing other diseases to manifest, or reduced ability to assimilate food or convert food to energy. The high Antarctic fish species *Trematomus bernacchii* has demonstrated acclimation to increased water temperatures, but a reduced growth up to 84% of mass and it is hypothesised that this is due to poor food conversion efficiency.[63]

Animal resilience, a built-in response to a particular pathogen type in the rarefied environment, can alternatively make endemic populations reservoirs. Unknown pathogens that reside in endemic species may affect trade-out, that is, trade in products coming from the polar regions. This is an understudied area. Recently, some evidence suggests that penguin species are the reservoir or maintenance species of Avian avulavirus species.[64] These viruses are not known quantities, with Wille et al. discovering a possible new species.[65] Their epidemiology is unknown though the role of the penguin appears key and it has been suggested that avulaviruses may spread into new hosts, affecting agricultural and livestock production and human health.[66] Newcastle disease virus is an avian avulavirus and has been responsible for outbreak epidemics in poultry across the world.[67] Different penguin populations have been found infected with the same species of avulavirus and so "potential carrier species, such as the kelp gull (*Larus dominicanus*), should be investigated. A more complete understanding of the broader geographic and host range of these viruses will enable a more accurate assessment of the potential for spread beyond Antarctica".[68]

2.3 Influences on emerging pathogens at the poles: Epidemiology of infectious disease

Various influences affect the rate of pathogenic transfer by movement of goods, people, and animals. The vast ice bodies in the high latitudes both North and South are increasingly under scrutiny for the effects that melting of that ice will have on the world's biosphere. In relation to disease transmission, the ability of international trade to balance proliferative pathogeneses against free trade remains for discussion.

2.3.1 Climate shift

"The impacts of climate change will depend on the rate of temperature changes and on the genotype and ecology of species. More negative impacts are expected in species physiologically specialised with respect to temperature and with limited acclimation capacity. Species living in thermostable environments are highly specialised within a narrow temperature range".[69]

Climate shift has been included in the list of possible transmission aides in the case of Pasteurellosis[70] as have moisture, temperature and habitat all of which are in turn affected by climate.[71] Pathogens are poleward moving such as *Vibrio* spp., others demonstrating genetic adaptations, for example, to increased carbon dioxide.[72] Transmission occurs through water as with Phocine Distemper Virus;[73] or through the cold upper atmosphere in masses of air as with *Polaromonas* spp.;[74] or in deep cold-water channels as with *Octadecabacter* between the poles.[75]

Given the emergence of pathogens in correlation to the warming environments of the Arctic and Antarctic, influences for increasing prevalence begin with examining the role of climate warming. The stable, homogenous and equilibrium of the high latitudes has meant its lower need to adapt to temperature challenges at levels associated with the proliferation and dispersion of pathogens. Yet as temperature increases, the resilience of the environment lowers, and the ability of pathogens from lower latitudes to survives increases. As Christiansen aptly puts it: "A putative disadvantage of specialized physiologies to frigid waters, however, is loss of genetic variability at adaptive loci[76] and a truncated flexibility to meet novel stressors, such as climate change and pollutants."[77]

Amongst the climate changes, increasing water temperatures are amongst the chief impacts. Not only will this affect the survival of

Northern fish species,[78] but also warmer water holds less oxygen and some pathogens benefit from this, for example, *Paramoeba perurans,* a parasite which causes amoeba gill disease (AGD) is salmon.[79] Not just a warming climate, but terrestrial warming is also an issue. A warming climate has been found responsible for the increased Northern proliferation of *Setaria tundra* in reindeer and moose in Northern Finland.[80] A century of parasitic research in Northern latitudes[81] has revealed "extreme weather events can result in the explosive emergence of disease leading to mortality and morbidity".[82] Patterns may emerge over a number of years featuring atypical high temperatures, which drive proliferation of pathogen and consequent host mortality events, which occurred in the case of *Setaria tundra* in reindeer.[83] Parasitic disease may prove to be a significant biomarker of polar health across the animal-human interface because it influences across both sustainability for populations of "diverse invertebrates, fishes, birds and mammals and...[affects] food security, quality and avail-ability for people".[84] Parasites ought to be included, as such, into wildlife population management and subsistence food security and safety, given their increase will also increase risk of exposure and infection for humans.[85] Food security in the High Arctic, for example, remains its own concern given that some microbial agents such as "the freeze-resistant *T. nativa* is the primary source for infections in people, through consumption of bears and walrus (*Odobenus rosmarus*)".[86]

The expansion of parasites in artiodactyla has been associated with cycles of glaciation,[87] the taxa's North expansion following the retreating ice throughout geographical history, for example, as with *Parelaphostrongylus odocoilei*.[88] In the case of *Setaria tundra,* the increase in parasitic-associated mortality occurs even though the species has been in the Holarctic throughout the Pliocene and Quaternary, through different episodic climate and geographic shifts.[89] This demonstrates that "temperature tolerances and resilience are critical...factors for distribution and persistence".[90] More broadly, an assessment of more than 600 crop pests (nematodes and insects) and pathogens since 1960 found an expansion towards the poles that is attributable to climate change.[91]

However, climate shift was not found to be a reason in declining musk oxen populations in the early 2000s.[92] This study demonstrated no significant pathologic findings upon post-mortem examination from any musk oxen adults or calf in the Western Alaska or Eastern North Slope regions, except the presence of copper, *Mycoplasma bovis, Echinococcus* spp., *Trueperella pyogenes,* and *Chlamydophila* in a number of individuals.[93] However, deaths were mostly due to bear predation or hoof lesions[94] presumably leading to either lameness and/or ascending infections or associated with copper deficiency:[95] "[p]redation contributed to 42% of deaths in the carcasses examined".[96]

2.3.2 Migrating animal species: Carriers, hosts, and vectors

Increased emergence of disease may be attributable to altered transmission rates (through altered frequency of interaction of or increased density of possible hosts) and altered host susceptibility due to lowered bodily resilience.[97] Translocation of animal species, either as vectors or hosts, and increased susceptibility of non-carrier animals (that is, animals which have disease) either directly or indirectly have a role in increasing the spread of disease. Warmer weather animals are being given expanded ranges, moving further North in the case of the Arctic, in particular, into areas previously dominated by endemic fauna such as polar bears.[98]

Migration to higher latitudes of the North and South is particularly evident in the shifting faunal boundary and the movement of fish species.[99] An inability of Antarctic or Arctic fish to move as they have evolved to exist at certain temperature ranges such as the absence of a heat-shock response in Antarctic notothenioids due to genetic depletion in response to living in a psychrophilic environment.[100] Fish migrate North as the water warms, temperature increases more profitable to those species from more temperate waters as well as faster growing species such as saffron cod over arctic cod.[101] The increasing translocation of fish species further North has been documented as boreal fish move into unexploited Northern waters[102] and there is increasing interaction at the Atlantic-Pacific fish interchange.[103] Sub-boreal species like boreal beaked redfish and the Arctic-boreal Bering flounder, will likely move North[104] and boreal Atlantic cod already inhabits the Barents Sea.[105] Among other species are increased frequency of movements of marine birds and mammals due to retreating sea ice between Atlantic and Pacific Oceans; there have been sightings of species in each basin not previously known to be there.[106] Northern Gannet and Manx Shearwater, usually restricted to the North Atlantic were seen in Alaska in 2011 for the former and the North Pacific for the latter.[107]

As temperatures warm, "[n]ew habitats will be colonized and distinct populations and species will mix as the reduced sea ice allows increased exchange across the Arctic".[108] Range expansion of temperate species into higher latitudes of the Arctic have been evidenced, for example, with *Mytilus* spp. mussels, with a demonstration of clear genetic difference between populations in Greenland and Eastern Atlantic of the same species of mussels, *Mytilus edulis*.[109] Other species have been found distinctly elsewhere such as *Mytilus trossulus* in high Arctic NW Greenland and *Mytilus galloprovincialis* in SW Greenland, Svalbard, and the Pechora Sea.[110] Evidence has also been found of hybridisation amongst mussel species in the High Arctic which may suggest adaptations over time to foster resilience.[111]

Range expansion is also true of pathogens, which translocate either along with their hosts, or in surrounding water and air. This will influence reciprocal exchange of parasites among different populations of hosts.[112] *Toxoplasma gondii* have been increasingly found in Arctic marine mammals and Phocine Distemper Virus, which historically affected Arctic dwelling seals, infect more temperate populations.[113] According to McKeon et al., the current era in the higher North is the "largest faunal exchange event to occur during the historical era".[114] Range expansions of, for example, *Aspergillus fumigatus,* a fungus isolate discovered in birds' nests in Antarctica, raised a question about the possible dispersal of this microbe (which is pathogenic to humans) by migratory bird species.[115]

Migrating vectors may take the form of a migrating animal or insects which are normally constrained geographically based on air and/or terrestrial thermoclines. Burek et al. ascribe the emergence of infectious disease to four factors, one of which is carrier host and vector range expansion.[116] Indeed, pathogens increase in range as "the insects and other vectors that carry them enter new ecological zones".[117]

2.3.3 Ballast water from ships

Polar shipping routes ("Polar Shipping routes") are on the increase.[118] Further sea-ice reduction coincides with and encourages increased transport by ships across the Arctic[119] with Antarctica set for the same trajectory. Shipping routes overlap with wildlife corridors.[120] The role of shipping companies, in particular, and the carriage of pathogens in ballast water, as anti-fouling and in shipping containers among crops, grain, and other goods that harbour pathogens will be carried into higher latitudes as ships push the boundaries of high latitudes both North[121] and South.

2.3.4 Fomite transfer and increased human activity

Increased human movement into the Arctic also increases the rate of spread, both by humans themselves and through industry, environment/

land use alterations, noise pollution through seismic activity,[122] and through engagement with animals previously naïve either to human habitations *in toto* or non-indigenous human habitations. For example, ungulate parasites have changed due to human-led introductions due to changing demographics: "human-mediated translocation, introduction and establishment of hosts and parasites over the past century have altered the distributions for helminths and other pathogens in some carnivores and ungulates".[123] These changing patterns of human movements and migration also have historical links and have affected infection pressures for pathogens where humans and animals come into contact.[124] In turn, this affects food security and safety, with increasing prevalence and altered transmission routes in traditional food sources such as muskoxen and caribou.[125]

2.3.5 Land use change

With a warming climate comes land use change, not just through extended shipping enterprises but also through the opening of mining, tourism and new food-production and agricultural initiatives:

> "the quest for petroleum and other hydrocarbons comprises two successive phases: search and extract. The latter phase is associated with biological consequences of leakages into the environment, hardly known for Arctic waters, and polar cod has become a sentinel species in studies of Arctic marine pollutants and their toxicity".[126]

In the Arctic petroleum exploration activities and fisheries, there are crucial new resilience-testers[127] and it has been found that adult female polar bears (*Ursus maritimus*) had various levels of contamination with organochlorine pesticides (OCPs) across the Arctic from regions of Svalbard, Franz Josef Land, Kara Sea, East Siberian Sea, and Chuckchi Sea.[128] The additional use of new technologies to monitor and aid reindeer migration as they are moved between pastures also is an additional burden.[129] This may be either due to overcrowding of reindeer herds and the associated increase in disease transmission rates[130] or possibly through increased human activity and fomite transfer.

a. Failure of harmonisation of food safety standards

Harmonisation of food safety standards is the aim of the Sanitary and Phytosanitary Measures (SPS)Agreement Article 3. This is discussed in Chapter 3 and refers broadly to the adoption by Members of standards based on the same standards, as approved by international bodies. The failure to have similar standards may result in the adoption of lower standards and resultant increasing pathogenic risk.

ZOONOSES IN THE ARCTIC

2.4 Zoonoses and the one health concern

The public health element of trading in disease, which is a current global concern, cannot be forgotten in the polar regions. Zoonoses (transmission of disease from animals to humans) is on the rise and in the endemic polar regions,[131] the effects of zoonoses between endemic animal populations and culturally distinct human populations may well become a significant human rights issue, given the current climate to protect indigenous and distinct cultural groups under protocols such as the United Nations Declaration on the Rights of Indigenous Peoples (UNDRIP). The zoonoses concern feeds back into the food security agenda of the WTO.[132] Emerging zoonoses is a primary concern of the World Health Organisation, which acknowledges that emerging zoonoses are due to "[e]nvironmental changes, human and animal demography, pathogen changes and changes in farming practice...food habits and religious beliefs...".[133] There is also a hypothesis that a lack of biodiversity increases the risk and incidence of zoonotic disease.[134]

Evidence for zoonotic transmission amongst the Arctic peoples has been emerging since the 1960s. Seven Eskimo were found to have Brucellosis infection (*B. melitensis* or *B. suis*) in a study published in 1963[135] and is still found in human population.[136] As all but two of the individuals had never left the area, transmission via external source was ruled out. Source of infection was deduced to be food-related: "The Eskimo in these areas relies to a large extent on fish, seal, caribou and reindeer for his food"[137] and ingest both the blood and marrow of ungulates. Eskimo were known to ingest raw meat, blood and bone marrow and whilst studies at the time were only suggestive, reindeer had known infection in Russia, caribou in Alaska, and caribou, moose and elk in various parts of Canada.[138] The importance of wild herds in the transmission of zoonoses was indicated by Toshach in 1963 when he stated as "control of Brucellosis in domestic animals... [becomes] more and more successful throughout the world, wild animal reservoirs as a source of human infection become suspect".[139]

Animals can be healthy even while being carriers, as has been shown in the case of reindeer carrying *E.coli* and methicillin-resistant *Staphylococcus aureus* (MRSA).[140] Infectious keratoconjunctivitis (IKC) is a major transmissible ocular disease in reindeer and has been associated with bacteria family Chlamydiaceae, some species being zoonotic.[141]

Protection only comes through hygiene standards at slaughter, where poor measures may mean the entry of zoonoses to "the food chain by direct or indirect fecal contamination".[142] In the study by Laaksonen et al., over 400 reindeer came from Northern Finland, located at or above 65 degrees N, and pathogens found included *Listeria monocytogenes* (in 3.2%), Yersinia (in 9.8%) and shiga-toxin producing *E. coli* (STEC, in 32.6%).[143] Wide infection was possibly due to corralling of animals.[144] This is of particular note where corralling and mass movement of animals on ever-increasing scales is part of food production.

Notes

1. Reisman, MW. Sovereignty and Human Rights in Contemporary International Law. 1990. *American Journal of International Law* 84: 866.
2. Larska, M., 2015. Pestivirus infection in reindeer (Rangifer tarandus). Front Microbiol 6, 1187–1187.
3. Ytrehus, B., Bretten, T., Bergsjo, B., Isaksen, K., 2008. Fatal pneumonia epizootic in musk ox (Ovibos moschatus) in a period of extraordinary weather conditions. EcoHealth 5, 213–223.
4. Duignan, P.J., Van Bressem, M-F., Baker, J.D., Barbieri, M., Colegrove, K.M., De Guise, S., de Swart, R.L., Di Guardo, G., Dobson, A., Duprex, W.P., Early, G., Fauquier, D., Goldstein, T., Goodman, S.J., Grenfell, B., Groch, K.R., Gulland, F., Hall, A., Jensen, B.A., Lamy, K., Matassa, K., Mazzariol, S., Morris, S.E., Nielsen, O., Rotstein, D., Rowles, T.K., Saliki, J.T., Siebert, U., Waltzek, T., Wellehan, J.F.X., 2014. Phocine distemper virus: Current knowledge and future directions. Viruses 6, 5093–5134.
5. Tryland, M., Neuvonen, E., Huovilainen, A., Tapiovaara, H., Osterhaus, A., Wiig, O., Derocher, A.E., 2005. Serologic survey for selected virus infections in polar bears at Svalbard. J Wildl Dis 41, 310–316.
6. Robertsen, G., Hansen, H., Bachmann, L., Bakke, T.A., 2007. Arctic charr (Salvelinus alpinus) is a suitable host for Gyrodactylus salaris (Monogenea, Gyrodactylidae) in Norway. Parasitology 134, 257–267.
7. Afema, J.A., Beckmen, K.B., Arthur, S.M., Huntington, K.B., Mazet, J.A.K., 2017. Disease complexity in a declining Alaskan Muskox (Ovibos Moschatus) population. Journal of Wildlife Diseases 53, 311–329.
8. Forde, T., Biek, R., Zadoks, R. et al. 2016. Genomic analysis of the multi-host pathogen *Erysipelothrix rhusiopathiae* reveals extensive recombination as well as the existence of three generalist clades with wide geographic distribution. BMC Genomics 17, 461. https://doi.org/10.1186/s12864-016-2643-0.

9. For example, see Handeland, K., Tengs, T., Kokotovic, B., Vikøren, T., Ayling, R.D., Bergsjø, B., Sigurðardóttir, Ó.G., Bretten, T., 2014. "Mycoplasma ovipneumoniae - A Primary Cause of Severe Pneumonia Epizootics in the Norwegian Muskox (Ovibos moschatus) Population" Plos One 9(9), e106116. https://doi.org/10.1371/journal.pone.0106116; Härkönen, T., Dietz, R., Reijnders, P., Teilmann, J., Harding, K., Hall, A., Brasseur, S., Siebert, U., Goodman, S.J., Jepson, P.D., Dau Rasmussen, T. & Thompson, P., 2006. "The 1988 and 2002 phocine distemper virus epidemics in European harbour seals" Diseases of Aquatic Organisms 68(2), 115–30.

10. das Neves, C.G., Roth, S., Rimstad, E., Thiry, E., Tryland, M., 2010. Cervid herpesvirus 2 infection in reindeer: A review. Veterinary Microbiology 143, 70–80.

11. Ibid.

12. Smits, S.L., Schapendonk, C.M.E., van Leeuwen, M., Kuiken, T., Bodewes, R., Stalin Raj, V., Haagmans, B.L., das Neves, C.G., Tryland, M., Osterhaus, A.D.M.E., 2013. Identification and Characterization of Two Novel Viruses in Ocular Infections in Reindeer. Plos One 8, e69711.

13. Larska, supra n 2.

14. das Neves et al., supra n 10.

15. Laaksonen, S., Oksanen, A., Julmi, J., Zweifel, C., Fredriksson-Ahomaa, M., Stephan, R., 2017. Presence of foodbore pathogens, extended-spectrum β-lactamase -producing Enterobacteriaceae, and methicillin-resistant Staphylococcus aureus in slaughtered reindeer in northern Finland and Norway. Acta veterinaria Scandinavica 59, 2–2.

16. Afema et al., supra n 7.

17. Vollmers, J., Voget, S., Dietrich, S., Gollnow, K., Smits, M., Meyer, K., Brinkhoff, T., Simon, M., Daniel, R., 2013. Poles Apart: Arctic and Antarctic Octadecabacter strains Share High Genome Plasticity and a New Type of Xanthorhodopsin. Plos One 8, e63422, 1.

18. Ibid., 10.

19. Ibid., 13.

20. Mykytczuk, N.C.S., Foote, S.J., Omelon, C.R., Southam, G., Greer, C.W., Whyte, L.G., 2013. Bacterial growth at −15°C; molecular insights from the permafrost bacterium Planococcus halocryophilus Orl. ISME J 7, 1211–1226.

21. Ciok, A., Budzik, K., Zdanowski, M.K., Gawor, J., Grzesiak, J., Decewicz, P., Gromadka, R., Bartosik, D., Dziewit, L., 2018. Plasmids of Psychrotolerant Polaromonas spp. Isolated From Arctic and Antarctic Glaciers - Diversity and Role in Adaptation to Polar Environments. Front Microbiol 9, 1285–1285, 1.

22. Ibid.

23. Ibid.

24. Shen, L., Liu, Y., Xu, B., Wang, N., Zhao, H., Liu, X., Liu, F., 2017. Comparative genomic analysis reveals the environmental impacts on two Arcticbacter strains including sixteen Sphingobacteriaceae species. Scientific Reports 7, 2055, 1

25. Ibid., 4.

26. Ibid., 8–10.

27. Townsend, A. K., Taff, C. C., Wheeler, S. S., Weis, A. M., Hinton, M. G., Jones, M. L., Logsdon, R. M., Reisen, W. K., Freund, D., Sehgal, R. N. M., Saberi, M., Suh, Y. H., Hurd, J., and Boyce, W. M. 2018. Low heterozygosity is associated with vector-borne disease in crows. *Ecosphere* 9(10), e02407. 10.1002/ecs2.2407.
28. Laaksonen et al., supra n 15, 10.
29. Ibid.
30. cited in Hueffer, K., O'Hara, T.M., Follmann, E.H., 2011. Adaptation of mammalian host-pathogen interactions in a changing arctic environment. Acta Veterinaria Scandinavica 53, 17–17. 5.
31. Burek, K.A., Gulland, F.M.D., O'Hara, T.M., 2008. Effects of Climate Change on Arctic Marine Mammal Health. Ecological Applications 18, S126–S134.
32. Christiansen, J.S., Mecklenburg, C.W., Karamushko, O.V., 2014. Arctic marine fishes and their fisheries in light of global change. Global Change Biology 20, 352–359.
33. Ibid.
34. Burek et al., supra n 31.
35. Duignan et al., supra n 4; Härkönen et al., supra n 9.
36. Follmann, E.H., Garner, G.W., Evermann, J.F., McKeirnan, A.J.,1996. Serological evidence of morbillivirus infection in polar bears (Ursus maritimus) from Alaska and Russia. Veterinary Record 138, 615–618.
37. Tryland et al., supra n 5.
38. Hoberg, E.P., Kutz, S., Galbreath, K., Cook, J., 2003. Arctic biodiversity: From discovery to faunal baselines—Revealing the history of a dynamic ecosystem. Journal of Parasitology 89, S84–S95. This exceptional work describes the host species and history of parasite migration across the holarctic during Pliocene and Pleistocene eras. It provides a starting point for knowing what parasites are currently found in hosts, which are linked to biogeographic history, and thus, can provide a reference against which expansion of range and host species can be measured.
39. Parker, J.R.C., Saunders, B.J., Bennett, S., DiBattista, J.D., Shalders, T.C., Harvey, E.S., 2019. Shifts in Labridae geographical distribution along a unique and dynamic coastline. Divers Distrib. 25, 1787–1799. https://doi.org/10.1111/ddi.12980; Arctic Ocean Diversity, http://www.arcodiv.org/Fish.html 3 August 2019.
40. Arctic Ocean Diversity http://www.arcodiv.org/Fish.html 3 August 2019
41. Christiansen, J.S., Reist, J.D., ABA, CAFF, chapter 6, 200, at https://www.arcticbiodiversity.is/about/index.php?option=com_content&view=article&id=8&Itemid=135 accessed 8 August 2020.
42. Neira, V., Tapia, R., Verdugo, C., Barriga, G., Mor, S., Ng, T.F.F., García, V., Del Río, J., Rodrigues, P., Briceño, C., Medina, R.A., González-Acuña, D., 2017. Novel Avulaviruses in Penguins, Antarctica. Emerg Infect Dis 23, 1212–1214; Wille, M., Aban, M., Wang, J., Moore, N., Shan, S., Marshall, J., González-Acuña, D., Vijaykrishna, D., Butler, J., Wang, J., Hall, R.J., Williams, D.T., Hurt, A.C., 2019. Antarctic Penguins as Reservoirs of Diversity for Avian Avulaviruses. Journal of Virology 93, e00271–00219.
43. Neira et al., supra n 42.
44. Ibid.

45. Wille et al., supra n 42.
46. Thomazelli, L.M., Araujo, J., Oliveira, D.B., Sanfilippo, L., Ferreira, C.S., Brentano, L., Pelizari, V.H., Nakayama, C., Duarte, R., Hurtado, R., Branco, J.O., Walker, D., Durigon, E.L., 2010. Newcastle disease virus in penguins from King George Island on the Antarctic region. Veterinary Microbiology 146, 155–160.
47. Vollmers et al., supra n 17, 7.
48. Ibid., 13.
49. Staley, J.T. & Gosink, J.J., 1999. Poles apart: biodiversity and biogeography of sea ice bacteria. Annual Review of Microbiology 53, 189–215.
50. Russo, R., Riccio, A., di Prisco, G., Verde, C., Giordano, D., 2010. Molecular adaptations in Antarctic fish and bacteria. Polar Science 4, 245–256.
51. Ibid.
52. Ibid.
53. Ibid., 247.
54. Chen, Z., Cheng, C.H., Zhang, J., Cao, L., Chen, L., Zhou, L., Jin, Y., Ye, H., Deng, C., Dai, Z., Xu, Q., Hu, P., Sun, S., Shen, Y., Chen, L., 2008. Transcriptomic and genomic evolution under constant cold in Antarctic notothenioid fish. Proceedings of the National Academy of Sciences of the United States of America 105, 12944–12949.
55. Russo et al., supra n 50, 248.
56. Ibid., 249.
57. Darcy, J.L., Lynch, R.C., King, A.J., Robeson, M.S., Schmidt, S.K., 2011. Global distribution of Polaromonas phylotypes—Evidence for a highly successful dispersal capacity. Plos One 6, e23742–e23742.
58. Ibid., 5.
59. Neira et al., supra n 42; Wille et al., supra n 42.
60. Wille et al., supra n 42.
61. Mora, A., García-Peña, F.J., Alonso, M.P., Pedraza-Diaz, S., Ortega-Mora, L.M., Garcia-Parraga, D., López, C., Viso, S., Dahbi, G., Marzoa, J., Sergeant, M.J., García, V., Blanco, J., 2018. Impact of human-associated Escherichia coli clonal groups in Antarctic pinnipeds: Presence of ST73, ST95, ST141 and ST131. Scientific Reports 8, 4678.
62. Ibid.
63. Sandersfeld, T., Davison, W., Lamare, M.D., Knust, R., Richter, C., 2015. Elevated temperature causes metabolic trade-offs at the whole-organism level in the Antarctic fish Trematomus bernacchii. The Journal of Experimental Biology 218, 2373–2381.
64. Wille et al., supra n 42.
65. Ibid., 5.
66. Ibid., 1.
67. Ibid., 2.
68. Ibid., 8.
69. Russo et al., supra n 50, 245.
70. Ytrehus et al., supra n 3, 219.
71. Laaksonen et al., supra n 15, 7.
72. Cavicchioli, R., Ripple, W.J., Timmis, K.N., Azam, F., Bakken, L.R., Baylis, M., Behrenfeld, M.J., Boetius, A., Boyd, P.W., Classen, A.T., Crowther, T.W., Danovaro, R., Foreman, C.M., Huisman, J., Hutchins, D.A., Jansson, J.K., Karl, D.M., Koskella, B., Mark Welch, D.B., Martiny, J.B.H.,

Moran, M.A., Orphan, V.J., Reay, D.S., Remais, J.V., Rich, V.I., Singh, B.K., Stein, L.Y., Stewart, F.J., Sullivan, M.B., van Oppen, M.J.H., Weaver, S.C., Webb, E.A., Webster, N.S., 2019. Scientists' warning to humanity: Microorganisms and climate change. Nature Reviews Microbiology 17, 569–586. https://doi.org/10.1038/s41579-019-0222-5.
73. Duignan et al., supra n 4.
74. Darcy et al., supra n 57.
75. Vollmers, supra n 17, 13.
76. Patarnello, T., Verde, C., di Prisco, G., Bargelloni, L., Zane, L., 2011. How will fish that evolved at constant sub-zero temperatures cope with global warming? Notothenioids as a case study. Bioessays, 33: 260–268. doi:10.1002/bies.201000124.
77. Christiansen, J.S., Mecklenburg, C.W., Karamushko, O.V., 2014. Arctic marine fishes and their fisheries in light of global change. Global Change Biology 20, 352–359, 356.
78. Reist, J.D., Wrona, F.J., Prowse, T.D., Power, M., Dempson, J.B., Beamish, R.J., King, J.R., Carmichael, T.J., Sawatzky, C.D., 2006. General effects of climate change on Arctic fishes and fish populations. Ambio 35, 370–380.
79. Hvas, M., Karlsbakk, E., Mæhle, S., Wright, D.W., Oppedal, F., 2017. The gill parasite Paramoeba perurans compromises aerobic scope, swimming capacity and ion balance in Atlantic salmon. Conserv Physiol 5, cox066–cox066.
80. Laaksonen et al., supra n 15, 10.
81. Hoberg et al., supra n 38, 9.
82. Ibid., 7.
83. Ibid.; Laaksonen et al., supra n 15.
84. Hoberg et al. supra n 38, 6.
85. Ibid., 10
86. Ibid., 27
87. Ibid., 48
88. Ibid., 53-4
89. Ibid., 49
90. Ibid., 56
91. Cavicchioli, et al. supra n 72.
92. Afema et al., supra n 7.
93. Ibid.
94. Ibid., 314–319.
95. Ibid., 326.
96. Ibid., 320.
97. Burek et al., supra n 31, S127–8.
98. Hueffer et al., supra n 30, 6.
99. Christiansen, J.S., Mecklenburg, C.W., Karamushko, O.V., 2014. Arctic marine fishes and their fisheries in light of global change. Global Change Biology 20, 352–359.
100. Russo et al., supra n 50, 247.
101. Helser, T.E., Colman, J.R., Anderl, D.M., Kastelle, C.R., 2017. Growth dynamics of saffron cod (Eleginus gracilis) and Arctic cod (Boreogadus saida) in the Northern Bering and Chukchi Seas. Deep Sea Research Part II: Topical Studies in Oceanography 135, 66.

102. Christiansen et al., supra n 99.
103. Wisz, M., Broennimann, O., Grønkjær, P., Moller, P., Olsen, S., Swinge-douw, D., Hedeholm, R., Nielsen, E., Guisan, A., Pellissier, L., 2015. Arctic warming will promote Atlantic–Pacific fish interchange. Nature Climate Change 5.
104. Christiansen et al., supra n 99.
105. Ibid.
106. McKeon, C.S., Weber, M.X., Alter, S.E., Seavy, N.E., Crandall, E.D., Barshis, D.J., Fechter-Leggett, E.D., Oleson, K.L.L., 2016. Melting barriers to faunal exchange across ocean basins. Global Change Biology 22, 465–473, 465. doi: 10.1111/gcb.13116.
107. Ibid., 467.
108. Ibid., 468.
109. Mathiesen, S.S., Thyrring, J., Hemmer-Hansen, J., Berge, J., Sukhotin, A., Leopold, P., Bekaert, M., Sejr, M.K., Nielsen, E.E., 2017. Genetic diversity and connectivity within Mytilus spp. in the subarctic and Arctic. Evolutionary Applications 10, 39–55.
110. Ibid.
111. Ibid.
112. Hoberg et al., supra n 38, 53.
113. McKeon et al., supra n 106, 470.
114. Ibid., 470.
115. de Sousa, J.R.P., Gonçalves, V.N., de Holanda, R.A., Santos, D.A., Bueloni, C., Costa, A.O., Petry, M.V., Rosa, C.A., Rosa, L.H., 2017. Pathogenic potential of environmental resident fungi from ornithogenic soils of Antarctica. Fungal Biol 121, 991–1000.
116. Burek et al., supra n 31.
117. FAO, The State of Food and Agriculture 2009: Livestock in the Balance, 2010. "Livestock and human and animal health", chapter 5, p 75 http://www.fao.org/3/i0680e/i0680e05.pdf accessed 20 December 2019.
118. Smith, L.C., Stephenson, S.R., 2013. New Trans-Arctic shipping routes navigable by midcentury. Proceedings of the National Academy of Sciences 110, 4871.
119. The Integrated Arctic Corridors Framework, Planning for responsible shipping in Canada's Arctic waters, 2016, https://www.pewtrusts.org/en/research-and-analysis/reports/2016/04/the-integrated-arctic-corridors-framework accessed 18 December 2019.
120. The Pew Charitable Trusts, 2016 found at Harry Wilson, "Mapping Arctic corridors; The Pew Charitable Trusts suggests shipping corridors in the Arctic that could be classified by level of risk", 2016 July 6, Canadian Geographic, https://www.canadiangeographic.ca/article/mapping-arctic-corridors accessed 18 December 2019.
121. Christiansen et al., supra n 99; Smith and Stephenson, supra n 118.
122. Christiansen et al., supra n 99, 356.
123. Hoberg et al., supra n 38.
124. Ibid.
125. Ibid.
126. Christiansen et al., supra n 99, 356.
127. Ibid.

128. Lie, E., Bernhoft, A., Riget, F., Belikov, S.E., Boltunov, A.N., Derocher, A.E., Garner, G.W., Wiig, Ø., Skaare, J.U., 2003. Geographical distribution of organochlorine pesticides (OCPs) in polar bears (Ursus maritimus) in the Norwegian and Russian Arctic. Science of the Total Environment 306, 159–170.
129. Larska, supra n 2.
130. Ibid.
131. Burek et al., supra n 31.
132. Grafton, QR, Daugbjerg, C & Qureshi, ME. Towards food security by 2050. 2015. *Food Security*, 7(2), 179–183.
133. "Emerging Zoonoses", World Health Organisation, https://www.who.int/zoonoses/emerging_zoonoses/en/ accessed 18 December 2019.
134. Ostfeld, R.S., 2009. Biodiversity loss and the rise of zoonotic pathogens. Clinical Microbiology and Infection: The official Publication of the European Society of Clinical Microbiology and Infectious Diseases 15 Suppl 1, 40–43.
135. Toshach, S., 1963. Brucellosis in the Canadian Arctic. Canadian Journal of Public Health/Revue Canadienne de Sante'e Publique 54, 271–275.
136. Yang, H.-X., Feng, J.-J., Zhang, Q.-X., Hao, R.-E., Yao, S.-X., Zhao, R., Piao, D.-R., Cui, B.-Y., Jiang, H., 2018. A case report of spontaneous abortion caused by Brucella melitensis biovar 3. Infectious Diseases of Poverty 7, 31.
137. Toshach, supra n 135, 272.
138. Ibid., 273.
139. Ibid., 274.
140. Laaksonen et al., supra n 15.
141. Sánchez Romano, J., Leijon, M., Hagström, Å., Jinnerot, T., Rockström, U.K., Tryland, M., 2019. Chlamydia pecorum Associated With an Outbreak of Infectious Keratoconjunctivitis in Semi-domesticated Reindeer in Sweden. Frontiers in Veterinary Science 6.
142. Laaksonen et al., supra n 15, 2.
143. Ibid., 5–6.
144. Ibid.

Suggested readings

Articles

Afema, J.A., Beckmen, K.B., Arthur, S.M., Huntington, K.B., Mazet, J.A.K., 2017. Disease complexity in a declining Alaskan Muskox (Ovibos Moschatus) population. Journal of Wildlife Diseases 53, 311–329.
Burek, K.A., Gulland, F.M.D., O'Hara, T.M., 2008. Effects of climate change on arctic Marine mammal health. Ecological Applications 18, S126–S134.
Cavicchioli, R., Ripple, W.J., Timmis, K.N., Azam, F., Bakken, L.R., Baylis, M., Behrenfeld, M.J., Boetius, A., Boyd, P.W., Classen, A.T., Crowther, T.W., Danovaro, R., Foreman, C.M., Huisman, J., Hutchins, D.A., Jansson, J.K., Karl, D.M., Koskella, B., Welch, M.D.B., Martiny, J.B.H., Moran, M.A., Orphan, V.J., Reay, D.S., Remais, J.V., Rich, V.I., Singh, B.K., Stein, L.Y.,

Stewart, F.J., Sullivan, M.B., van Oppen, M.J.H., Weaver, S.C., Webb, E.A., Webster, N.S., 2019. Scientists' warning to humanity: Microorganisms and climate change. Nature Reviews Microbiology 17, 569–586. https://doi.org/10.1038/s41579-019-0222-5.

Chen, Z., Cheng, C.H., Zhang, J., Cao, L., Chen, L., Zhou, L., Jin, Y., Ye, H., Deng, C., Dai, Z., Xu, Q., Hu, P., Sun, S., Shen, Y., Chen, L., 2008. Transcriptomic and genomic evolution under constant cold in Antarctic notothenioid fish. Proceedings of the National Academy of Sciences of the United States of America 105, 12944–12949.

Christiansen, J.S., Mecklenburg, C.W., Karamushko, O.V., 2014. Arctic marine fishes and their fisheries in light of global change. Global Change Biology 20, 352–359.

Christiansen, J.S., Reist, J.D., ABA, CAFF, chapter 6, 200, at https://www.arcticbiodiversity.is/about/index.php?option=com_content&view=article&id=8&Itemid=135 accessed 8 August 2020.

Ciok, A., Budzik, K., Zdanowski, M.K., Gawor, J., Grzesiak, J., Decewicz, P., Gromadka, R., Bartosik, D., Dziewit, L., 2018. Plasmids of psychrotolerant polaromonas spp. Isolated from arctic and Antarctic glaciers—diversity and role in adaptation to polar environments. Front. Microbiol. 9:1285. doi: 10.3389/fmicb.2018.01285.

Darcy, J.L., Lynch, R.C., King, A.J., Robeson, M.S., Schmidt, S.K., 2011. Global distribution of polaromonas phylotypes—evidence for a highly successful dispersal capacity. PloS one 6, e23742–e23742.

das Neves, C.G., Roth, S., Rimstad, E., Thiry, E., Tryland, M., 2010. Cervid herpesvirus 2 infection in reindeer: A review. Veterinary Microbiology 143, 70–80.

Davidson, R,K, Handeland, K, Kapel, C.M., 2008. High tolerance to repeated cycles of freezing and thawing in different Trichinella nativa isolates. Parasitol. Res. 103, 1005–1010.

de Sousa, J.R.P., Gonçalves, V.N., de Holanda, R.A., Santos, D.A., Bueloni, C., Costa, A.O., Petry, M.V., Rosa, C.A., Rosa, L.H., 2017. Pathogenic potential of environmental resident fungi from ornithogenic soils of Antarctica. Fungal Biol 121, 991–1000.

Duignan, P.J., Van Bressem, M-F., Baker, J.D., Barbieri, M., Colegrove, K.M., De Guise, S., de Swart, R.L., Di Guardo, G., Dobson, A., Duprex, W.P., Early, G., Fauquier, D., Goldstein, T., Goodman, S.J., Grenfell, B., Groch, K.R., Gulland, F., Hall, A., Jensen, B.A., Lamy, K., Matassa, K., Mazzariol, S., Morris, S.E., Nielsen, O., Rotstein, D., Rowles, T.K., Saliki, J.T., Siebert, U., Waltzek, T., Wellehan, J.F.X., 2014. Phocine distemper virus: Current knowledge and future directions. Viruses 6, 5093–5134.

Follmann, E.H., Garner, G.W., Evermann, J.F., McKeirnan, A.J., 1996. Serological evidence of morbillivirus infection in polar bears (ursus maritimus) from Alaska and russia. Veterinary Record 138, 615–618.

Forde, T., Biek, R., Zadoks, R. et al. 2016. Genomic analysis of the multi-host pathogen *Erysipelothrix rhusiopathiae* reveals extensive recombination as well as the existence of three generalist clades with wide geographic distribution. BMC Genomics 17, 461. https://doi.org/10.1186/s12864-016-2643-0.

Grafton, Q.R., Daugbjerg, C., Qureshi, M.E. Towards food security by 2050. 2015. Food Security, 7(2), 179–183.

Härkönen, T., Dietz, R., Reijnders, P., Teilmann, J., Harding, K., Hall, A., Brasseur, S., Siebert, U., Goodman, S.J., Jepson, P.D., Dau Rasmussen, T., Thompson, P., 2006. The 1988 and 2002 phocine distemper virus epidemics in European harbour seals. Diseases of Aquatic Organisms 68, 115–130.

Helser, T.E., Colman, J.R., Anderl, D.M., Kastelle, C.R., 2017. Growth dynamics of saffron cod (Eleginus gracilis) and Arctic cod (Boreogadus saida) in the Northern Bering and Chukchi Seas. Deep Sea Research Part II: Topical Studies in Oceanography 135, 66.

Hoberg, E.P., Kutz, S., Galbreath, K., Cook, J., 2003. Arctic biodiversity: From discovery to faunal baselines—revealing the history of a dynamic ecosystem. Journal of Parasitology 89, S84–S95.

Hueffer, K., O'Hara, T.M., Follmann, E.H., 2011. Adaptation of mammalian host-pathogen interactions in a changing arctic environment. Acta Veterinaria Scandinavica 53, 17. https://doi.org/10.1186/1751-0147-53-17.

Hvas, M., Karlsbakk, E., Mæhle, S., Wright, D.W., Oppedal, F., 2017. The gill parasite paramoeba perurans compromises aerobic scope, swimming capacity and ion balance in Atlantic salmon. Conserv Physiol 5, cox066.

Laaksonen, S., Oksanen, A., Julmi, J., Zweifel, C., Fredriksson-Ahomaa, M., Stephan, R., 2017. Presence of foodborne pathogens, extended-spectrum β-lactamase-producing Enterobacteriaceae, and methicillin-resistant Staphylococcus aureus in slaughtered reindeer in northern Finland and Norway. Acta Veterinaria Scandinavica 59, 2.

Larska, M., 2015. Pestivirus infection in reindeer (Rangifer tarandus). Front Microbiol 6, 1187.

Lie, E., Bernhoft, A., Riget, F., Belikov, S.E., Boltunov, A.N., Derocher, A.E., Garner, G.W., Wiig, Ø, Skaare, J.U., 2003. Geographical distribution of organochlorine pesticides (OCPs) in polar bears (Ursus maritimus) in the Norwegian and Russian Arctic. Science of The Total Environment 306, 159–170.

Mathiesen, S.S., Thyrring, J., Hemmer-Hansen, J., Berge, J., Sukhotin, A., Leopold, P., Bekaert, M., Sejr, M.K., Nielsen, E.E., 2017. Genetic diversity and connectivity within Mytilus spp. in the subarctic and Arctic. Evolutionary Applications 10, 39–55.

McKeon, C.S., Weber, M.X., Alter, S.E., Seavy, N.E., Crandall, E.D., Barshis, D.J., Fechter-Leggett, E.D., Oleson, K.L.L., 2016. Melting barriers to faunal exchange across ocean basins. Global Change Biology 22, 465–473. doi: 10.1111/gcb.13116.

Mora, A., García-Peña, F.J., Alonso, M.P., Pedraza-Diaz, S., Ortega-Mora, L.M., Garcia-Parraga, D., López, C., Viso, S., Dahbi, G., Marzoa, J., Sergeant, M.J., García, V., Blanco, J., 2018. Impact of human-associated Escherichia coli clonal groups in Antarctic pinnipeds: Presence of ST73, ST95, ST141 and ST131. Scientific Reports 8, 4678.

Mykytczuk, N.C.S., Foote, S.J., Omelon, C.R., Southam, G., Greer, C.W., Whyte, L.G., 2013. Bacterial growth at −15°C; Molecular insights from the permafrost bacterium Planococcus halocryophilus Or1. ISME J 7, 1211–1226.

Neira, V., Tapia, R., Verdugo, C., Barriga, G., Mor, S., Ng, T.F.F., García, V., Del Río, J., Rodrigues, P., Briceño, C., Medina, R.A., González-Acuña, D., 2017. Novel Avulaviruses in penguins, Antarctica. Emerg Infect Dis 23, 1212–1214.

Ostfeld, R.S., 2009. Biodiversity loss and the rise of zoonotic pathogens. Clinical Microbiology and Infection: The Official Publication of the European Society of Clinical Microbiology and Infectious Diseases 15 Suppl. 1, 40–43.

Parker, J.R.C., Saunders, B.J., Bennett, S., DiBattista, J.D., Shalders, T.C., Harvey, E.S. 2019. Shifts in labridae geographical distribution along a unique and dynamic coastline. Diversity and Distributions. 25: 1787–1799. https://doi.org/10.1111/ddi.12980.

Patarnello, T., Verde, C., di Prisco, G., Bargelloni, L., Zane, L. 2011, How will fish that evolved at constant subzero temperatures cope with global warming? Notothenioids as a case study. Bioessays, 33, 260–268. doi:10.1002/bies.201000124.

Reist, J.D., Wrona, F.J., Prowse, T.D., Power, M., Dempson, J.B., Beamish, R.J., King, J.R., Carmichael, T.J., Sawatzky, C.D., 2006. General effects of climate change on arctic fishes and fish populations. Ambio 35, 370–380.

Robertsen, G., Hansen, H., Bachmann, L., Bakke, T.A., 2007. Arctic charr (Salvelinus alpinus) is a suitable host for Gyrodactylus salaris (Monogenea, Gyrodactylidae) in Norway. Parasitology 134, 257–267.

Russo, R., Riccio, A., di Prisco, G., Verde, C., Giordano, D., 2010. Molecular adaptations in Antarctic fish and bacteria. Polar Science 4, 245–256.

Sánchez Romano, J., Leijon, M., Hagström, Å, Jinnerot, T., Rockström, U.K., Tryland, M., 2019. Chlamydia pecorum associated with an outbreak of infectious keratoconjunctivitis in semi-domesticated reindeer in Sweden. Frontiers in Veterinary Science 6.

Sandersfeld, T., Davison, W., Lamare, M.D., Knust, R., Richter, C., 2015. Elevated temperature causes metabolic trade-offs at the whole-organism level in the Antarctic fish Trematomus bernacchii. The Journal of Experimental Biology 218, 2373–2381.

Shen, L., Liu, Y., Xu, B., Wang, N., Zhao, H., Liu, X., Liu, F., 2017. Comparative genomic analysis reveals the environmental impacts on two Arcticibacter strains including sixteen Sphingobacteriaceae species. Scientific Reports 7, 2055.

Smith, L.C., Stephenson, S.R., 2013. New trans-Arctic shipping routes navigable by midcentury. Proceedings of the National Academy of Sciences 110, 4871.

Smits, S.L., Schapendonk, C.M.E., van Leeuwen, M., Kuiken, T., Bodewes, R., Stalin Raj, V., Haagmans, B.L., das Neves, C.G., Tryland, M., Osterhaus, A.D.M.E., 2013. Identification and characterization of Two novel viruses in ocular infections in reindeer. Plos One 8, e69711.

Staley, J.T., Gosink, J.J., 1999. Poles apart: Biodiversity and biogeography of sea ice bacteria. Annual Review of Microbiology 53, 189–215.

Thomazelli, L.M., Araujo, J., Oliveira, D.B., Sanfilippo, L., Ferreira, C.S., Brentano, L., Pelizari, V.H., Nakayama, C., Duarte, R., Hurtado, R., Branco, J.O., Walker, D., Durigon, E.L., 2010. Newcastle disease virus in penguins from King George Island on the Antarctic region. Veterinary Microbiology 146, 155–160.

Toshach, S., 1963. Brucellosis in the Canadian Arctic. Canadian Journal of Public Health/Revue Canadienne de Sante'e Publique 54, 271–275.

Townsend, A.K., Taff, C.C., Wheeler, S.S., Weis, A.M., Hinton, M.G., Jones, M.L., Logsdon, R.M., Reisen, W.K., Freund, D., Sehgal, R.N.M., Saberi, M., Suh, Y.H., Hurd, J., Boyce, W.M. 2018. Low heterozygosity is associated with vector-borne disease in crows. Ecosphere 9 (10), e02407. 10.1002/ecs2.2407.

Tryland, M., Neuvonen, E., Huovilainen, A., Tapiovaara, H., Osterhaus, A., Wiig, O., Derocher, A.E., 2005. Serologic survey for selected virus infections in polar bears at Svalbard. J Wildl Dis 41, 310–316.

Vollmers, J., Voget, S., Dietrich, S., Gollnow, K., Smits, M., Meyer, K., Brinkhoff, T., Simon, M., Daniel, R., 2013. Poles apart: Arctic and Antarctic Octadecabacter strains share High genome plasticity and a New type of Xanthorhodopsin. Plos One 8, e63422.

Wille, M., Aban, M., Wang, J., Moore, N., Shan, S., Marshall, J., González-Acuña, D., Vijaykrishna, D., Butler, J., Wang, J., Hall, R.J., Williams, D.T., Hurt, A.C., 2019. Antarctic penguins as reservoirs of diversity for avian avulaviruses. J Virol 93:e00271–19. https://doi.org/10.1128/JVI.00271-19.

Wisz, M., Broennimann, O., Grønkjær, P., Moller, P., Olsen, S., Swingedouw, D., Hedeholm, R., Nielsen, E., Guisan, A., Pellissier, L., 2015. Arctic warming will promote Atlantic–Pacific fish interchange. Nature Climate Change 5.

Yang, H.-X., Feng, J.-J., Zhang, Q.-X., Hao, R.-E., Yao, S.-X., Zhao, R., Piao, D.-R., Cui, B.-Y., Jiang, H., 2018. A case report of spontaneous abortion caused by Brucella melitensis biovar 3. Infectious Diseases of Poverty 7, 31.

Ytrehus, B., Bretten, T., Bergsjo, B., Isaksen, K., 2008. Fatal pneumonia epizootic in musk ox (Ovibos moschatus) in a period of extraordinary weather conditions. EcoHealth 5, 213–223.

Other:

Arctic Ocean Diversity http://www.arcodiv.org/Fish.html 3 August 2019.

"Polar Shipping routes", The Geography of Transport Systems, The spatial organization of transportation and mobility, https://transportgeography.org/?page_id=412 accessed 18 December 2019.

The Integrated Arctic Corridors Framework, Planning for responsible shipping in Canada's Arctic waters, 2016, https://www.pewtrusts.org/en/research-and-analysis/reports/2016/04/the-integrated-arctic-corridors-framework accessed 18 December 2019.

The Pew Charitable Trusts, 2016 found at Harry Wilson, "Mapping Arctic corridors; The Pew Charitable Trusts suggests shipping corridors in the Arctic that could be classified by level of risk", 2016 July 6, Canadian Geographic, https://www.canadiangeographic.ca/article/mapping-arctic-corridors accessed 18 December 2019.

"Emerging Zoonoses", World Health Organisation, https://www.who.int/zoonoses/emerging_zoonoses/en/ accessed 18 December 2019.

FAO, The State of Food and Agriculture 2009: Livestock in the Balance, 2010. "Livestock and human and animal health", chapter 5, p 75 http://www.fao.org/3/i0680e/i0680e05.pdf accessed 20 December 2019.

3 Applying the SPS protocol

This chapter applies the application of the standards required to apply a measure that restricts the trade in animal-based products as applied to food safety standards, where such measures can satisfy an exception to the non-discriminatory market access approach of the WTO. Such measures must fall within the general exception to trade recognised by the SPS Agreement[1] where measures protecting plant, animal or human life or health are allowed. Basic entitlements under the SPS Agreement include the ability to "take sanitary and phytosanitary measures necessary for the protection of human, animal or plant life or health" (Article 2.1).

Such measures are viable as long as the measure is "based on scientific principles" (Article 2.2) and does not impose arbitrary discrimination between members of similar prevailing conditions (Article 2.3), provided that such measures are not inconsistent with the provisions of this Agreement. They must also abide by the requirements for risk assessment and accord with the international standards as set by organisations such as "Codex Alimentarius Commission, the International Office of Epizootics, and the international and regional organizations operating within the framework of the International Plant Protection Convention" (Article 3.4) and must be

> "...adapted to the sanitary or phytosanitary characteristics of the area — whether all of a country, part of a country, or all or parts of several countries — from which the product originated and to which the product is destined. In assessing the sanitary or phytosanitary characteristics of a region, Members shall take into account, inter alia, the level of prevalence of specific diseases or pests, the existence of eradication or control programmes, and appropriate criteria or guidelines which may be developed by the relevant international organizations". (Article 6.1)

Australia-Apples (AB)[2] stated "while Article 5.1 directs a Member conducting a pest risk assessment to take into account internationally developed risk assessment techniques, this does not mean that a risk assessment must be based on or conform to such techniques. Nor does it imply that compliance with such techniques alone suffices to demonstrate compliance with a Member's obligations under the SPS Agreement" (para 246). Thus, while national members must adopt measures to the SPS characteristics of a country and its areas, the techniques for assessing those measures are not stipulated for strict adherence.

SETTING THE STANDARDS: FOOD AND SAFETY STANDARDS FOR IMPORTATION AND EXPORTATION

3.1 International legal and policy instruments

Under the Agreement, three main bodies are recognised for being responsible for setting standards relevant to the application of sanitary and phytosanitary measures curtailing the international trade in goods. These bodies are recognised in the preamble to the Agreement:

"Desiring to further the use of harmonized sanitary and phytosanitary measures between Members, on the basis of international standards, guidelines and recommendations developed by the relevant international organizations, including the Codex Alimentarius Commission, the International Office of Epizootics, and the relevant international and regional organizations operating within the framework of the International Plant Protection Convention, without requiring Members to change their appropriate level of protection of human, animal or plant life or health".

This acknowledgement of the abilities of these organisations is reinforced and codified more specifically in the Agreement itself:

Article 3.4: Members shall play a full part, within the limits of their resources, in the relevant international organisations and their subsidiary bodies, in particular, the Codex Alimentarius Commission, the International Office of Epizootics, and the international and regional organisations operating within the framework of the International Plant Protection Convention, to promote within these organisations the development and periodic review of standards, guidelines and recommendations with respect to all aspects of sanitary and phytosanitary measures.

As far as animal products are concerned, the Office of Epizootics (OIE) and the Codex Alimentarius Commission (CAC) are more relevant. This is not to say that guidelines protecting the trade in plants is not relevant, as part of the epidemiology of several agents of disease in animals requires the presence of certain types of plants, on which the larvae develop, as with the development of liver fluke, for example.[3] In fact, there are more organisations which play a role in developing applicable international standards relevant to standards for trade in animals and animal products. These include those mentioned, CAC and the OIE, and also, the Food and Agriculture Organisation (FAO) and the World Health Organisation (WHO), the latter take an active role in setting standards for food safety. The FAO, the WHO and the OIE established a tripartite Memorandum of Understanding to work together on issues in food health, security and safety in 2018.[4] Given as Article 3.4 refers to "relevant international organizations", these additional bodies are included in the ambit of the provision, and hence, measures for the importation of food products by Members must accord with these international standards (Article 3.4 SPS). They also must be "…adapted to the sanitary or phytosanitary characteristics of the area … from which the product originated and to which the product is destined" (Article 6.1 SPS). Such systems have been built to prevent the spread and build capability for monitoring and evaluation over trade in animals and animal products. Systems of surveillance both national and international have been set up to increase the collection and aggregation of data relating to disease emergence and those areas which have, for example, disease-free status.

International standards applicable to the trade and transport of animal and animal products, within the context of the SPS Agreement, fall to the World Organisation for Animal Health (OIE) under Annex A(3) (b). It is one of the three organisations acknowledged for maintenance of international standards in the SPS Agreement. One of the roles of the OIE is harmonisation between Members (*India-Agricultural Products, AB* 4.14).[5] Description of harmonisation and a further discussion on standard-setting are provided later. In the context of the poles, where standard-setting has, in terms of global trade, not considered the endemic nature of the poles, this is the more apt place to proceed.

STANDARDS ASSESSMENT: NAÏVE ENVIRONMENT OF THE POLES

This section examines the allowable restrictions on trade in the context of the endemic Arctic and Antarctic, that is, restrictions to be placed on Arctic and Antarctic products. Endemism of the Arctic and Antarctic gives it a fragility and lowered resilience to new pathogens, including food-borne pathogens. The concern of paramount importance here is whether, in order to satisfy trade egalitarianism, the standards for health and trade in food will be lowered (Silverglade 2000, 6).[6] Trade prohibitions on animal products both to and from the Arctic and Antarctic need to take account of these regions as endemic regions of natural wilderness of their own value. The requirements for assessing trade restrictions as a result even where mandated by the Agreement to be based on scientific available evidence, and the assessment of measures, cannot be applied in the same manner. Given the unknown effect of many vectors, hosts and diseases in a warming climate, the use of precaution ought to be center-focus (discussed below). Indeed perhaps, it is plausible to have trade restrictions specifically based on an approach of 'unknown effect' rather than proven effect, which would result in a new standard away from the scientific sufficiency model currently used in the SPS Agreement. The concern about lowering international health standards to satisfy trade egalitarianism is especially true in the Arctic and Antarctic.[7]

3.2 Article 6: Endemism in the context of the poles

Adaptation to regional conditions, including pest- or disease-free areas and areas of low pest or disease prevalence

1 Members shall ensure that their sanitary or phytosanitary measures are adapted to the sanitary or phytosanitary characteristics of the area — whether all of a country, part of a country, or all or parts of several countries — from which the product originated and to which the product is destined. In assessing the sanitary or phytosanitary characteristics of a region, Members shall take into account, inter alia, the level of prevalence of specific diseases or pests, the existence of eradication or control programmes, and appropriate criteria or guidelines which may be developed by the relevant international organisations.

2 Members shall, in particular, recognise the concepts of pest- or disease-free areas and areas of low pest or disease prevalence. Determination of such areas shall be based on factors such as geography, ecosystems, epidemiological surveillance, and the effectiveness of sanitary or phytosanitary controls.

3 Exporting Members claiming that areas within their territories
are pest- or disease-free areas or areas of low pest or disease
prevalence shall provide the necessary evidence thereof in order
to objectively demonstrate to the importing Member that such
areas are, and are likely to remain, pest- or disease-free areas
or areas of low pest or disease prevalence, respectively. For this
purpose, reasonable access shall be given, upon request, to the
importing Member for inspection, testing and other relevant
procedures.

Recognition of the poles in so far as recognising that these regions
require specific measures for the prohibition of trade due to their
inherent endemic status, is in the endemic area provisions of Article
6. However, the overriding tenor of the Article seems to be to validate
disease-free products leaving an area. The focus is on encouraging
fair and free market access of products from countries which declare
that areas are pest- or disease-free, that is, to ensure the demarcation
of areas which have a reduced level of trade barrier. Demarcation of
disease-free areas in the context of exporting animal products may
be premature and also miss the mark in so far as protection of these
unique areas is concerned: for the latter, the focus for the preservation of the unique status of the polar regions needs to focus on
restrictions of the importing nations, based on factors such as geography, ecosystems, and epidemiological surveillance. The lack of
available and full scientific evidence as regards the disease status of
these regions, and also the lack of better scientific evidence regarding
the impact of translocated pathogens are only just emerging more
clearly.

Of particular importance to the polar regions is the specification of
consideration of "the level of prevalence of specific diseases or pests"
in Article 6.1. On its own, this provision should serve as a bulwark to
unnecessary entry of pathogens into the endemic regions (and out of)
where certain pathogens extant in some Members are not to be found
in polar regions.

In the *Australia-Apples* case, we see another safety net. In that case,
Australia was prevented from refusing importation to New Zealand
Apples on the basis of a zero risk threshold because their policy did
not itself specify the need for a zero risk threshold, rather one that
reduced the threat to minimal. In the case of the poles, where a zero
risk policy ought to be adopted, any panel assessing complaints

against restrictions will need to take into consideration (and enforce) a zero risk policy.

However, the history of Article 6 might encourage a reading restricted to disease-free zones or areas of low prevalence, as between areas free of disease and those not free of disease in *one* country (*Russia-Pigs*, para 5.63).[8] If applied in this restricted way, the question is how useful is this provision, read in this way, to the Arctic and Antarctic.

Future contestation in the Antarctic is, as regards the law, a more interesting issue. Where no protective zone over the remaining wilderness areas of Antarctica can be agreed under the Convention on the Conservation of Antarctic Marine Living Resources (CCAMLR), use of the continent for exploration remains open. An influx of workers, with unknown knowledge of the region or its laws and carrying unknown disease with potential transmission or deposition in a naive environment, leaves wide open the import of food-borne pathogens with unknown effect.

Cases discussed in relation to Article 6 are not in relation to endemic regions, which may curtail their relevance. However, they include discussion of the parameters specifically related to restrictions of imports coming from disease-free, pest-free or low prevalence areas.

Article 6 needs to be read holistically (*India-Agricultural Products, AB*).[9] Specifically, the "failure to recognize and determine that disease-free area, and to adapt its SPS measure accordingly, is inconsistent with Articles 6.1 and 6.2 only if that exporting Member can also establish that it took the steps prescribed in Article 6.3" (*Russia-Pigs, AB*, para 5.97; *India-Agricultural Products, AB*, para. 5.156). Articles 6.1 and 6.2 are connected (*Russia-Pigs, AB*) and refer to the importing countries duties, while Article 6.3 refers to the exporting members duties (*Russia-Pigs, AB*, para 5.62). Trade into the Arctic and Antarctic requires examination of Articles 6.1 and 6.2. Article 6.3 refers to the exporting Member obligations; so, in the context of the polar regions, it relates to trade-out of Antarctica or the Arctic. Reading Article 6 accurately, at least in a way that "recognizes the concepts of "disease-free areas" and "areas of low disease prevalence"" (*India-Agricultural Products, AB*, para 3.1(c)(ii)), has been a major issue in both the *India-Agricultural* case and the *Russia-Pigs* case. It is an obligation of the importing Member that it recognises the concept of disease/pest freedom or disease/pest low prevalence, specifically because in so doing, it may distinguish or set apart those areas of a country or region that are not affected by an outbreak of pestilence (*Russia-Pigs, AB*).

3.2.1 Articles 6.1 and 6.2

Article 6.1 states the overarching obligation; that any SPS measure must be adapted to the SPS characteristics of the originating area and the destination area (*Russia-Pigs,* paras 5.46, 5.96). This requirement for adaptation is an ongoing obligation (*India-Agricultural Products; Russia-Pigs,* para 5.121), which requires Members to dynamically reassess their measures in relation to the disease status (*Russia-Pigs,* para 5.121; *India-Agricultural Products*, AB, para 5.132).

Article 6.1 needs to be adapted to regional conditions (*Russia-Pigs*, AB, para 5.92) and products cannot be banned without a risk assessment (ibid., para 5.87). The subarticle is satisfied where accordance with both sentences is observed: the first sentence requires adaptation of SPS measures to "the SPS characteristics of the area from which a product originated and of the area to which the product is destined" (*Russia-Pigs*, AB, para 5.96) and second sentence needs those SPS characteristics of the relevant area/s assessed with a "view to adapting its measures accordingly" (ibid.).

In the case of *Russia-Pigs*, the Appellate Body stated, "...we consider that the process of adaptation to regional SPS characteristics pursuant to Article 6 requires that the importing Member evaluate all the relevant evidence concerning the areas that an exporting Member claims are pest- or disease-free or of low pest or disease prevalence. This evaluation is addressed by the second sentences of Articles 6.1 and 6.2 of the SPS Agreement..." (*Russia-Pigs,* AB, para 5.91). Under the second sentence, a Member must assess "the SPS characteristics of the relevant areas with a view to adapting its measures accordingly" (*Russia-Pigs*, AB, para 5.96). The panel found that a Member may fall fowl of Article 6.1 where a "Member's regulatory regime precludes the recognition of such concept" as pest- or disease-free or low prevalence (*Russia-pigs*, AB, para 5.91). In *India-Agricultural Products*, the SPS measures at issue were not adapted to the SPS characteristics of the areas of origination due to a failure to recognise the concept of areas of disease-freedom or low prevalence under Article 6.2. In addition, there has been no risk assessment, thus violating both the first sentence and second sentence of the article, respectively (para 5.128).

Article 6.1 has a link to Article 6.3 and in some instances, may rely on the latter in order to be satisfied (though there are exceptions mentioned in *India-Agricultural Products*, and recognised in *Russia-Pigs* AB, para 5.107).

In relation to the polar regions, the application of Article 6.1 depends on the characterisation of the SPS characterisation of the areas, either as a whole, or partitioned according to geographic, national, or other boundaries. The open question is whether such SPS characterisation may include a type of disease-freedom not consonant with test-and-proof but rather on scientific understanding of naïve status (both as precaution and in lieu of evidence, as collection of evidence may involve violation of naïve status).

A reading of Article 6.2, the prominent Article of Article 6, must be read in accordance with both Article 6.1 and also the title and subheading of the Article (*India-Agricultural Products*, AB, para 5.133). Such a reading indicates that ""pest- or disease-free areas" and "areas of low pest or disease prevalence" are a subset of all the SPS characteristics of an area that may call for the adaptation of an SPS measure. We read the words "in particular", together with the title to Article 6, as underlining the interlinkages between the first and second paragraphs of Article 6. More specifically, we consider that these elements point to the particular saliency of "pest- or disease-free areas" and "areas of low pest or disease prevalence" as factors to be taken into account in assessing the SPS characteristics of a region, pursuant to the second sentence of Article 6.1. These considerations, in our view, indicate that, together, Articles 6.1 and 6.2 accord prominence to the content of Article 6.2 as one particular way through which a Member can ensure that its SPS measures are "adapted", as required by Article 6.1" (*India-Agricultural Products,* AB, para 5.133).

The Appellate Body in the *India-Agricultural Products* case queried the use of the word "adaptation" in relation to an SPS measure and that it presupposed the recognition of the concept of pest or disease free/low prevalence areas. In particular, the recognition of the concepts would require an affirmative act "*distinct from* and *taken prior to* the adoption of an SPS measure. In our view, this does not seem entirely consistent with the Panel's statement that there is no prescribed format for the recognition of the concepts and that it is the prerogative of Members to decide how to do so" (*India - Agricultural Products*, AB, para 5.143). Recognition of pest- or disease-free areas may be done in different ways (*Russia-Pigs*, AB, para 5.127). This notion of regionalisation is more than just an abstract idea (*Russia-Pigs,* AB, para 5.138) and must be recognised in fact (*Russia-Pigs,* AB, para 5.131). Not everything will require an affirmative act (*Russia-Pigs*, AB, para 5.128) and "what an exporting Member must objectively demonstrate depends on the specific disease and on the situation in the particular area at issue" (para 5.47). Legal analysis of what the de facto recognition of regionalisation meant, was not completed by the Appellate Body as the issues required to resolve the question not completely addressed by the participants in front of the panel including "probative value of the evidence" (*Russia-Pigs*, AB, para 5.141). Article 6.2 elaborates upon Article 6.1 in so far as SPS measures are adapted to the SPS characteristics of the area of origin and destination (*Russia-Pigs*, AB, para 5.135). The major factors pivotal in the Article are threefold. "Shall" and "in particular" relate to a particular subset of SPS characteristics under Article 6.1 (*Russia-Pigs*, AB, para 5.121) and in Article 6.1, the use of "ensure", whilst requiring application of measures consistently and systematically, grants an amount of latitude in not specifying a certain manner in which to apply SPS measures (*Russia-Pigs*, AB, 5.124). Second, the second sentence notion of determination is to be based on several factors (*Russia-Pigs*, AB, para 5.125). The list is reiterated in *Russia-Pigs:* "(i) geography; (ii) ecosystems; (iii) epidemiological surveillance; (iv) effectiveness of SPS controls; (v) level of prevalence of specific diseases or pests; (vi) existence of eradication or control programmes; and (vii) information corresponding to appropriate criteria or guidelines developed by the relevant international organizations" (para 5.47). Third, as mentioned above, the recognition of disease- or pest-free areas or those of low prevalence may be done in different ways. Where (iii) through to (vii) involves human presence and scientific evaluation based on in-situ examination, again this runs foul of naïve environment protection.

Where a Member has failed to recognise pest- or disease-free areas or those areas of low prevalence of pest or disease, as required under Article 6.2, first sentence, leads to the inevitable conclusion that the second sentence has also been breached because distinguishing features have not been utilised to recognise the difference in areas (*India-Agricultural Products*, AB, para 5.123). In *India-Agricultural Products*, India's relevant legislation prohibited trade in relevant products on a country-wide basis, which contradicted the need to recognise disease freedom/low prevalence (para 5.126).

"The above passages from the Panel Report show, in our view, that the distinction between the obligation to "recognize" and the obligation to "implement" is one created by India, and not one that is reflected in the Panel's findings. To reiterate, the Panel did not opine on whether the obligation to "recognize" under Article 6.2 requires the implementation of a legal instrument in domestic law. Nor did the Panel find an inconsistency with Article 6.2

on the basis that India had failed to "implement" the concept of disease-free areas. Rather, the Panel correctly found that, since... [the measure] *contradicts* the requirement to recognize the concepts of disease-free areas and areas of low disease prevalence India's...[avian influenza] measures, "taken together", do not recognize these concepts with respect to AI, as required by Article 6.2 of the SPS Agreement". (*India-Agricultural Products*, AB, para 5.175)

Article 6.2 must be considered in the light of Article 6.3, specifically that the exporting country has an opportunity of making a claim that areas are pest- or disease-free or of low prevalence, and that this opportunity is operational (*Russia-Pigs*, AB, paras 5.129 and 5.142). Whilst customs controls and OIE codes may be useful, they are not relevant for operationalisation of the subarticle (*Russia-Pigs*, para 5.146), but administrative practice may be indicative (*Russia-Pigs*, AB, para 5.150). Importing members may assess evidence including through on-site inspection (*Russia-Pigs*) again, the third place which runs counter to an avoidance strategy for naïve environments which would be the most effective method for ensuring the preservation of naïve environment. This is to the exclusion of those peoples who have lived in the environment, without moving from it, for generations as they are effectively part of the environment. New visitors carry, for example, enteropathogens unknown to individual biomes across species in the new host environment.[10]

3.2.2 Article 6.3

Article 6.3 stands apart from Articles 6.1 and 6.2 (*India-Agricultural Products*, AB, para 5.121). Exporting from an endemic area begins with examination of Article 6.3 specifically where "an exporting Member claims that areas within its territory are pest- or disease-free or of low pest or disease prevalence"(*Russia-pigs*, para 5.96). *Russia-Pigs* made it clear that Article 6.3 only comes into play at the time when an exporting Member claims areas of pest- or disease-free (or low prevalence) (para 5.96) and then satisfaction of Articles 6.1 and 6.2 must be observed (ibid.). The obligation rests with the exporters to prove products are clean, that is, provide "the necessary evidence" in support of its claim "in order to objectively demonstrate to the importing Member" that the relevant areas "are, and are likely to remain, pest- or disease-free or of low pest or disease prevalence" (*Russia-Pigs*, para 5.61).

Article 6.1 may be used to inform a determination of whether an exporting Member has recognised pest- or disease-free or low prevalence areas (objectively demonstrated using the information required for an assessment of SPS characteristics under Article 6.1), but nothing denotes this to be strictly necessary (*India-Agricultural Products*, AB, para 5.120 and 5.158). Whether the Arctic or Antarctic will be able to make a claim for disease-freedom or more likely, where increasing pathogens result from unknown transmission, epidemiology and virulence, whether these nations will satisfy this provision, will impact upon a Member's ability to be an exporter.

The first sentence of Article 6.3 relates to exporting members in terms of being able to objectively assess the nature, quantity and quality of the evidence (*Russia-Pigs*, AB, para 5.70), but this specifically does not apply to importation (*Russia-Pigs,* AB, para 5.70). Importation requirements are met in reading the second sentences of Articles 6.1 (re SPS characteristics) and 6.2 (determining pest or disease status) (*Russia-Pigs*, AB, para 5.71). All evidence needs to be evaluated and verified by an importing nation (*Russia-Pigs*, AB, para 5.62) and to this end, access needs to be given to requesting importing nations for purposes of assessing whether measures are adapted to SPS characteristics of area (*Russia-Pigs*, AB, para 5.61). Again, "where relevant, the importing Member may analyse data gathered through on-site visits to the area concerned and rely upon any other information that it may have acquired from other sources, including from competent international organizations" (ibid., 5.62).

Such international organisations' guidelines include "Article 5.3.7(d) of the Terrestrial Code, which requires an importing Member to "determine ... whether it accepts an area as a zone for the importation of animal products"" (*Russia-pigs*, footnote 192). However, the importing Member's evaluation of the relevant evidence is *not* covered by Article 6.3, which addresses the "duties that apply to ... *exporting* Members". (*Russia-Pigs*, AB, para 5.62). An importing Member's ""determination" of the pest or disease status of a given area is addressed by the second sentence of Article 6.2, and forms part of that Member's "assess[ment]" of the SPS characteristics of that area within the meaning of the second sentence of Article 6.1" (*Russia-Pigs,* AB, para 5.59 and 5.60).

The fulcrum of Article 6.3 turns on the understanding of "necessary evidence" and "likely to remain so".

a Necessary evidence

Necessary means that which can be demonstrated not to be "excessive or not pertinent to a determination by the importing Member with respect to the pest or disease status of the relevant area" (*Russia-Pigs,* AB, para 5.64). Evidence may include that collected from on-site visits or from international organisations (*Russia-Pigs,* AB, para 5.71), and also includes "testimony, documents and tangible objects that...tend to prove or disprove the existence of an alleged fact" (*Russia-Pigs,* AB, para 5.63 using the dictionary definition from *Black's Law Dictionary*, 7th ed., B.A. Garner (Ed.) West Group, 1999, p. 578).

Evidence provided by an exporting Member to an importing Member must be of a "nature, quantity, and quality sufficient to enable the importing Member's authorities ultimately to make a determination as to the pest or disease status of the relevant areas within the exporting Member's territory" (*Russia-Pigs,* AB, para 5.66). Thus, the aim of the evidence is to demonstrate the pest or disease status of the Member (*Russia-Pigs,* AB, para 5.63). A panel review of compliance is limited to this *(Russia-Pigs,* AB, para 5.66). Evidence is required to be particularised to:

> "the pest or disease and the area concerned, and cannot merely adduce generic information or unsubstantiated assertions...this evidence may encompass laboratory-type scientific information (e.g. the pathogenicity of a given disease) and/or technical information about the situation on the ground (e.g. the effectiveness of SPS controls in place in the area covered by the exporting Member's claim)...(as well as the) non-exhaustive list of factors enumerated in the second sentence of Article 6.2 – including geography, ecosystems, epidemiological surveillance, and the effectiveness of SPS controls – may shed light on the type of evidence that an exporting Member is expected to provide under Article 6.3". (*Russia-Pigs,* AB, para 5.63)

A Member's appropriate level of protection (ALOP) may inform the nature, quantity, and quality of the evidence that an exporting Member is expected to provide in order to make the objective demonstration provided for in Article 6.3 (*Russia-Pigs,* AB, para 5.65). Importantly, Russia's claims in the *Russia-Pigs* case makes an interesting point that time needs to be considered in the evaluation of compliance, specifically that "what constitutes a "reasonable" time period depends on various factors including: the timespan that has elapsed between the disease outbreak and the "regionalization" request; the expansion of disease-free areas and/or the establishment of new disease-free areas; the differences in veterinary services and geography between exporting countries; whether the exporting country is dealing with an outbreak for the first time or has already accumulated experience from prior outbreaks; and whether, during the importing Member's evaluation, disease outbreaks occur in the alleged disease-free areas" (para 5.77).

Time periods are not adequately considered in the SPS Agreement, with Annex C (1)(a) to the Agreement the only stipulation that "Members to "ensure, with respect to any procedure to check and ensure the fulfilment of [SPS] measures, that...such procedures are undertaken and completed without undue delay"" (*Russia-Pigs*, AB, para 5.81).

An exporting member needs to have "necessary evidence" that is, evidence tending to "prove or disprove the existence of an alleged fact" (*Russia-Pigs*, AB, para 5.63, using Black's law Dictionary). This definition was from 1999 according to the reference. Advances in diagnostic ability have been made however and are continual and necessary evidence disproving or proving the definitive disease presence let alone status is an evolving field. First, disease presence does not indicate prevalence and prevalence may be considered only one aspect of disease status. Proof and disproof is built over time, very often after significant protocols have been adhered to for clinical research, including ethics protocols, which may take substantial time and are rigorous. Veterinary proof/disproof is based on Koch's postulates which requires its own significant satisfaction/dissatisfaction of proofs. Thus, the question of whether there exists "necessary proof or disproof" is a matter of timing. The more important question is whether exportation should be enabled where disease-status and determinative prevalence are still unknown and yet deductive reasoning allows us to consider with scientific maturity that there may in fact be a rising disease prevalence occurring. In this regard, the law, as in the past, falls behind the science, it being utilised as a stagnant tool of application rather than as dynamic response to changing science.

It may be a benefit that in the *Russia-Pigs* case, the panel agreed that firstly, the list of factors in Article 6.2 (including ecosystems, geography, epidemiological surveillance and SPS controls) was non-exhaustive and that "the situation on the ground (e.g. the effectiveness of SPS controls in place in the area covered by the exporting Member's claim)" was relevant (para 5.63). However, the assertion in the same paragraph that "an exporting Member is expected to provide *particularized evidence* with respect to the pest or disease and the area concerned, *and cannot merely adduce generic information or unsubstantiated assertions*" seems, scientifically at least, onerous particularly given that, within the meaning of science, proof and disproof carry such a heavy burden. This relies very much on the ability of those hearing cases to adjudge fairly, with consideration of both the science and the law, the SPS measure in question, the legal basis for it, and the scientific information available.

"Necessary" refers to the ability of an importing member to make an assessment of the SPS characteristics of an area, based on the objective demonstration by the exporting member, taking account of the nature, quantity, quality of the evidence which may be shown in the ALOP (*Russia-Pigs*, AB, paras 5.64–5.65). Necessary may be informed by Articles 6.1 and 6.2 (second sentences) (*Russia-Pigs*, AB, para 5.65). The panel recuses itself in this case (*Russia-Pigs*) from a scientific mandate, stating "[h]owever, a panel assessing compliance with Article 6.3 is not called upon to determine for itself, based on the evidence provided by the exporting Member, whether the relevant areas are, and are likely to remain, pest- or disease-free or of low pest or disease prevalence" (para 5.66); however, it is a nonsense that a panel can determine whether evidence was sufficiently delivered to an importing Member without some knowledge of whether that evidence was of sound enough scientific value to enable an importing Member to make an objective determination of whether disease- or pest-free areas were likely to remain so. That is, a panel cannot adjudge whether the evidence delivered was of due weight, as regards the disease- or pest-free area, unless it understands the scientific value of the evidence. Secondly, in an altering climate, it is not certain that even scientific evidence to date can predict whether previously disease- or pest-free areas are likely to remain so. This qualification is difficult and cumbersome. It may have been better to make a determination based on, firstly, the volume of evidence provided and, secondly, whether any absence of information was warranted given a changing climate.

In *Russia-Pigs*, the Appellate body did not complete the legal analysis of the mechanism to determine whether a country may recognise the concepts of disease-free, pest-free or areas of low pest or disease prevalence nor did the panel prescribe a particular *manner* in the *India-Agricultural Products* case for how to recognise pest-free, disease-free or low prevalence areas. Where intricate science is involved in understanding food-borne pathogens and zoonotic disease, there is an inability to either accurately portray such by legal representatives or be adjudged by legal minds.

b Likely to remain so

SPS measures must be dynamic and adaptable over time (*India-Agricultural Products*, AB, para. 5.157.) The Appellate Body has noted that this requirement "is an ongoing obligation that applies *upon* adoption of an SPS measure as well as thereafter" (ibid.). Referring back to Article 6, SPS measures must be "adapted to regional SPS characteristics, and that the nature of that obligation" is not static, but rather ongoing...[and] adjusted over time so as to establish and maintain their continued suitability"" (*India-Agricultural Products*, AB, paras 126–127).

3.3 Article 2: The right to restrict trade

Basic rights and obligations

1 Members have the right to take sanitary and phytosanitary measures necessary for the protection of human, animal or plant life or health, provided that such measures are not inconsistent with the provisions of this Agreement.

2 Members shall ensure that any sanitary or phytosanitary measure is applied only to the extent necessary to protect human, animal or plant life or health, is based on scientific principles and is not maintained without sufficient scientific evidence, except as provided for in paragraph 7 of Article 5.

3 Members shall ensure that their sanitary and phytosanitary measures do not arbitrarily or unjustifiably discriminate between Members where identical or similar conditions prevail, including between their own territory and that of other Members. Sanitary and phytosanitary measures shall not be applied in a manner which would constitute a disguised restriction on international trade.

4 Sanitary or phytosanitary measures which conform to the relevant provisions of this Agreement shall be presumed to be in accordance with the obligations of the Members under the provisions of GATT 1994 which relate to the use of sanitary or phytosanitary measures, in particular the provisions of Article XX(b).

3.3.1 Article 2.1

At its broadest reading, Article 2.1 sets up this provision as a protection for the Arctic countries as able to restrict trade where SPS measures are made to protect the human, animal, or plant life or health. However, the subarticles 2.2 and 2.3 place qualifications upon this allowability; the question is whether the qualifications undermine the performance of the protection offered in the context of the polar regions.

The second part of Article 2.1, in particular, is problematic for the polar regions: it undermines the specific application to endemic regions where (i) disease zoning is not present, and (ii) equivalence under Article 4 cannot be met (discussed later). The polar regions represent a new area of application for the SPS protocol more generally. Consideration of Article 6 as it relates to Article 2.1 may well be the defining relational difficulty in this context.

Possible or probably clash of 2.3 with Article 6 and the precautionary principle requires some discrimination to take place. The provision within the Article of the words "where identical or similar conditions prevail" has been applied to market access. But can this equally be used for other conditions, namely, ecosystem differences? Environment or human rights differences? The SPS Agreement does not consider restrictions based on human rights or environment (Kennedy, 2000; 87)[11], where food safety links with livelihood, market access, and local trade (either impacted through intra-country trade or disease). It brings to the fore the decades long clash between international trade and international environmental codes. Secondly, how will or how can the exception under Article XX(b) be utilised for the advantage of the Arctic and Antarctic endemic ecosystem? In this context, what will be seen as the new trade restrictions – radiation, quarantine, inspection procedures? Where these place higher cost and technical burdens on countries?

3.3.2 Article 2.2

Article 2.2 is a complicated article, pivoting on current judicial delineation of the concepts of "to the extent necessary", what "based on scientific principles" means, and what is sufficiency of scientific evidence. Article 2.2 has a history of being both read with, against and as a counterpoint to sections of Article 5. These make the general application of Article 2.2 confusing in relation to the polar regions, particularly where SPS measures are already in place and may include a measure of precautionary approach.

a To the extent necessary

Application of the first requirement of Article 2.2 cannot be discussed without reference to its counterparts in Article 5.6 (*Australia-Apples*, AB, para 339). An SPS measure needs to be applied only to the extent necessary to protect human, animal, or plant life or health, but the delineation of "extent necessary" is to be further understood examining Article 5.6 (*India-Agricultural Products*, PR, para 7.613.), which provides that SPS measures be "no more trade-restrictive than required to achieve" the relevant objectives. This particular provision is set to become more complex in application as regards evolving scientific understanding. For example, the trade in food products requires an understanding in disease process, transmission, aetiology and pathogenicity. Where pathogenicity is unknown, exact measures to curb the spread of disease may not be completely effective. Further, where there are asymptomatic carriers, parameters based on inspection may not have the requisite sensitivity.

b Based on scientific principles and
maintained with sufficient scientific evidence

Article 2.2 seeks to maintain open trade corridors. Fundamentally, this is problematic when there is no scientific evidence which either supports or denies trade restrictions. In an endemic area which is undergoing dramatic shifts in geomorphology and resilience both of its land and animal species, the lack of scientific evidence ought to work in favour of restricting trade for the benefit of ensuring human, animal, and plant life and health. However, the history of application of the SPS protocol vis-a-vis trade measures does not support this.

Maintaining a measure must have sufficient scientific evidence which has been held to mean the "scientific evidence must bear a rational relationship to the measure, be sufficient to demonstrate the extent of the risk which the measure is supposed to address, and be of the kind necessary for a risk assessment" (*US-Poultry*, PR, para. 7.200).[12] The qualifier "sufficient" in relation to scientific evidence demonstrates the need for an "adequate relationship between two elements, *in casu*, between the SPS measure and the scientific evidence" (*Japan-Agricultural Products II*, AB, para 73). This may not be as accurate as an understanding or interpretation of the provision. Sufficient is an adjective in the phrase, adjoining "scientific evidence". The text of the subarticle refers to sufficient scientific evidence, thus not quantifying a specific volume or amount of scientific evidence required, only that it is "sufficient".

By scientific standards proof of pathogenicity of an organism, for example, must fulfil Koch's postulates: pathogen "isolation from a diseased organism, growth of the agent in pure culture, and the development of disease when the virus is re-introduced into a healthy organism" (Prescott, Feldmann & Safronetz 2017, 2).[13] There must be sufficient studies and evidence, therefore, to be able to fulfil the requirement in order to state that a pathogen causes a disease.

The text of Article 2.2 reads, "sanitary or phytosanitary measure... is based on scientific principles and is not maintained without sufficient scientific evidence..." and this may make the argument more coherent that sufficiency of scientific evidence may be based on scientific principles. Alternatively, the use of a scientific principle such as the precautionary principle which covers the flaws of trade liberality where there is a lack of scientific understanding or research *ab initio*, may be supplanted via this interpretation. Adhering to *Japan-Agricultural Products II* reasoning that the sufficiency spoken of is relational and refers to adequacy of the relationship between the scientific evidence and the SPS measure may favour a broad reading whereby the SPS measure relates adequately to the evidence and vice versa is deemed sufficient for validation. However, it also leaves wide the prospect of a very narrow reading that where scientific evidence is lacking and a measure is highly restrictive that the relational concept no longer satisfies the sufficiency or relatedness goal. Given as Article 2.2 specifically refers to scientific principles being used as the basis for measures, a cleaner reading would be using the words as written, that is, that there needs to be sufficient evidence. Where there is only anecdotal evidence, the sufficiency standard may not be met if read strictly within this framework.

However, two benefits may come from interpreting the provision in this manner. Firstly, it may encourage national bodies to invest in research into those pathogens encroaching into the Arctic and Antarctic, placing a restriction at first and arguing that the conditions for sufficiency are being met. The provision provides that a measure cannot be "*maintained* without sufficient scientific evidence" (emphasis added) and so there is an argument here that a provision may be put in place prior to a sufficiency of scientific evidence. Second, there is the possibility that, where these provisions become to be read in light of human and environmental principles, sufficiency of scientific evidence may be considered secondary to the proof that a measure is based on scientific principles (including the precautionary principle). Thus, the interpretation of Article 2.2 matures in line with scientific deduction and evidence.

Despite the Appellate Body in *Japan-Agricultural Products II* (para 82) finding that an insufficiency cannot be limited in scope to where scientific evidence is clearly insufficient, this does not exclude the argument that situations where evidence is *absent* will not fall fowl of the sufficiency standard. Indeed, in *Japan-Apples*, scientific evidence excludes both unsubstantiated information and hypotheses which have not been demonstrated (paras 8.92–8.93, 8.98). This is an issue where discovery of new pathogeneses is often by chance and at first substantiated by anecdotal evidence. More broadly, it could be argued that where the SPS construes scientific evidence in a manner to restrict a nation's *prima facie* right to safeguard its resources, wildlife and health, even based on initial anecdotal evidence, there is a breach of national sovereignty. Deference to national safeguarding measures has been appreciated in the *EC-Hormones* case, where the panel, in determining sufficiency of scientific evidence to warrant the maintenance of an SPS measure, "may, of course, and should, bear in mind that responsible, representative governments commonly act from perspectives of prudence and precaution where risks of irreversible, e.g. life-terminating, damage to human health are concerned" (*EC-Hormones*, AB, para 124).[14] Further, where there is no relevant scientific studies or reports in existence, the burden would then arguably pass to the respondent (*Japan-Agricultural Products II*, AB, para 137).

The idea of sufficiency has been dealt with simultaneously to considering scientific evidence, the latter being the type of information acquired through the scientific evaluation, considering the vector, transmission route and likely survival of the bacteria (*Japan-Apples,* AB, para 145).[15] Negligible risk was identified by the panel, but it was based on scientific evidence (known transmission etc.). As such the measure was seen as "clearly disproportionate" to the risk (*Japan-Apples*, PR, para 8.198).[16]

In *India-Agricultural Products*, the scientific basis was considered to be evidence with "the necessary scientific and methodological rigour to be considered reputable science…the correctness of the views need not have been accepted by the broader scientific community, the views must be considered to be legitimate science according to the standards of the relevant scientific community" (AB, para 5.28).

The interesting argument advanced by Japan for Article 2.2 was for a reading that allowed a degree of discretion to the importer on the manner of evaluation of scientific evidence (AB, para 150).

""the historical facts of trans-oceanic expansion of the bacteria" and the rapid growth of international trade, and which is premised on "the fact that the pathways of … transmission of the bacteria are still unknown in spite of several efforts to trace them"—is reasonable as well as scientific because it is derived from "perspectives of prudence and precaution"". (AB, para 150 quoting appellant submission para 73 and para 81, latter quote the *EC-Hormones*, AB para 124)

The *Japan-Apples* case involved fire blight in apples. Action was based around what was normally exported – usually mature, symptomless apples were the norm (AB, para 160) and this meant a prima facie case that an SPS measure was not maintained with sufficient scientific evidence (AB, para 167). The measure was disproportionate to the risk (para 163) because the US only exported mature, symptomless apples (para 160). The Appellate Body Report in *Japan-Agricultural Products II* stated as follows a much referred statement:

> "Whether there is a rational relationship between an SPS measure and the scientific evidence is to be determined on a case-by-case basis and will depend upon the particular circumstances of the case, including the characteristics of the measure at issue and the quality and quantity of the scientific evidence". (para 84; cited in *Japan-Apples* AB, para 162; *Japan-Apples, PR*, para 8.103)

Evaluation of evidence is a matter for the panel in a dispute as "the trier of facts; they enjoy a margin of discretion in assessing the value of the evidence, and the weight to be ascribed" (*Japan-Apples*, AB, para 166). They are not required to give precedence to importer's evaluation of scientific evidence and risk and can instead consider the opinion of scientific expertise (ibid.). The question of who is an expert remains unclear particularly when expertise ought to be both disease-based and geographically- or location-based. Knowledge of pathogenesis may be useful and which the Appellate Body has read broadly: in *Japan-Apples*, the Appellate Body found that "it sufficed for the United States to address only the question of whether mature, symptomless apples could *serve as a pathway for fire blight*" (para 131, emphasis added).

The sufficiency standard of Article 2.2 needs to be read in conjunction with Articles 5.1 (requirement for risk assessment), 3.3 and 5.7. Article 2.2 requires a "rational or objective relationship between the SPS measure and the scientific evidence" (*Japan-Agricultural Products*, AB, para 74). Here, we shall look at the relationships between Article 2.2 and the related provisions of Article 5.

3.3.3 Article 2.2 and Article 5.7

Article 5.7 may be used to justify provisional measures used by a Member where there is insufficient scientific evidence. There is also a sufficiency measure to Article 5.7 that where there is insufficient scientific evidence to perform a risk assessment, the Member "shall seek to obtain the additional information necessary for a more objective assessment of risk and review the sanitary or phytosanitary measure accordingly within a reasonable period of time", which may include seeking an expert opinion (*Australia-Apples,* AB, para 240). A violation of Article 5.7 where a measure is not based on sufficient scientific evidence, including that provided for determining sufficiency under Article 5.7, will constitute a violation of Article 2.2 (*Russia-Pigs,* PR, para 7.718).[17] In the *Russia-Pigs* case, the Russian argument was that the Panel had "overlooked the difference between the general requirement to provide some form of a valid veterinary certificate … with the specific requirements contained in the EU-Russia bilaterally negotiated veterinary certificates" (cited in the report of the AB, para 5.15). Bilaterally negotiated veterinary certificates were found to be secondary to the WTO rights and obligations (*Russia-Pigs,* PR, para 5.34). Finally, the sufficiency standard has been connected to Article 3.3, which allows a higher level of protection where there is scientific justification.[18]

3.3.4   Article 2.2 and Articles 5.1, 5.2

Article 2.2 also bears a relationship with Articles 5.1 and 5.2. Article 2.2 is to be constantly read in conjunction with Article 5.1 (*EC-Hormones,* AB, para 180). The requirement that an SPS measure must be based on scientific evidence and sufficient scientific evidence under Article 2.2, also informs the basis of the risk assessment required under Article 5.1 (*Australia-Apples,* AB, para 209). Following this, Article 5.2 requires the risk assessment to take consideration of relevant scientific evidence (*Australia-Apples,* AB, paras 206–208). Whether a "risk assessment is a proper risk assessment within the meaning of Article 5.1 and Annex A(4) must be determined by assessing the relationship between the conclusions of the risk assessor and the relevant available scientific evidence" (*Australia-Apples,* AB, para 208).

Case law would indicate that these subparagraphs of Article 5 are, in a sense, subsidiary provisions with more information on determination of a violation of Article 2.2. Article 2.2 is broader in scope that either Article 5.1 or 5.2 so that a violation of Articles 5.1 and/or 5.2 will mean a violation of Article 2.2, but "not all instances of violation of Article 2.2 entail a violation of Articles 5.1 and 5.2" (*India-Agricultural Products,* AB, para 5.7). *Australia-Apples* found that "by maintaining an import prohibition … in violation of Article 5.1, Australia has, *by implication,* also acted inconsistently with Article 2.2 of the *SPS Agreement*…there is a one-way, dependent relationship in law between the more specific provisions of Article 5.1 or Article 5.2, on the one hand, and the more general provisions of Article 2.2, on the other hand" (cited in *India-Agricultural Products,* AB, para 5.23). However, in *India-Agricultural Products,* it was stated that where a measure was not based on a risk assessment as per Articles 5.1 and 5.2, there was a presumption, albeit not a definitive determination, that there was a violation of Article 2.2 (*India-Agricultural Products,* AB, para 5.23).

In *India-Agricultural Products,* India argued that the original Panel had erred in finding inconsistency with Article 2.2 as a "consequence of its finding that they (India's measures) are inconsistent with Articles 5.1 and 5.2" (para 5.2). India relied upon the international standards delivered in the OIE Terrestrial Code in lieu of a risk assessment, a situation which resulted in the panel's finding that "India's [Avian Influenza]...measures are not based on a risk assessment and that they are therefore inconsistent with Articles 5.1 and 5.2, the Panel further found that India's AI measures are inconsistent with Article 2.2 because they are not based on scientific principles and are maintained without sufficient scientific evidence" (para 5.10).

However, reading Articles 5.1 and 2.2 in conjunction is based on risk assessments needing to support the SPS measure (*India-Agricultural Products,* AB, para 5.16). Risk assessments are mandatory, denoted by the use of the word "shall" and "based on", which requires an objective relationship that "persists and is observable between an SPS measure and a risk assessment" (*India-Agricultural Products,* AB, para 5.16). A risk assessment is to include not just experimentally perceived risks but also "the actual potential for adverse effects on human health in the real world where people live and work and die" (*EC-Hormones* AB, para 187). Following *Australia-Salmon,*[19] *India-Agricultural Products* notes that where an SPS measure is not based on a risk assessment the measure "*can be presumed, more generally,* not to be based on scientific principles or to be maintained without sufficient scientific evidence" (para 5.23). Use of an expert does not negate the need to abide by the requirements of Articles 5.1 and 5.2 (*Australia-Apples* AB, para 244).

3.3.5 *Article 2.2 and Article 5.6*

Similarly, an SPS measure found inconsistent with Article 5.6 may presuppose an inconsistency with Article 2.2 (*India-Agricultural Products,* AB, para 5.37).

3.3.6 *Article 2.3*

Article 2.3 has three phrases which are, both absolutely and in their collaborative reading with other articles, pivotal for curtailing trade which may pose a threat to the endemic polar regions: "arbitrarily or unjustifiably discriminate"; "identical or similar conditions"; and "disguised restriction on international trade". In case of read on the basis of trade terms and market access only, Article 2.3 poses a grave threat to the polar regions. However, in case of read in conjunction with a reading of Article 6 and giving due acknowledgement of the right to quarantine endemic zones, Article 2.3 may serve to lead the way in enabling necessary restrictions on trade where endemism is threatened and where there is less than adequate scientific evidence. The possible hindrance to this is the interpretation and weight given to the second sentence of Article 2.3; "[s]anitary and phytosanitary measures shall not be applied in a manner which would constitute a disguised restriction on international trade."

a Not arbitrary or unjustifiably discriminatory

According to Kennedy 2000 (84), Article 2.2 and 2.3 must be satisfied in order for a measure not to be considered unjustifiable or discriminatory, regardless of its adherence to the remainder of the GATT. Any prohibition, to be justified must be based on scientific principles and evidence. Of course, the question arises in the context of the poles, where scientific evidence is not in abundance, as to what trade restrictions are to be applied: does one look to the precautionary principle to preserve the unique ecosystem; or does one look to protect liberal trade by arguing for trade based on *current* scientific best practice? The latter is the gold standard for veterinary medical procedures, skill and knowledge, but to what extent this should influence movements of goods which have far greater implications is another matter. Indeed, "many scientific determinations require judgments among competing scientific views" (Kennedy 2000, 85). Of course, "standards, guidelines, and recommendations developed by the Codex, OIE, and IPPC that have a major trade impact are to be monitored" (Kennedy 2000, 85) and such international codes may serve a vital function in justifying trade restrictions. Importantly, such a use of these codes does not justify a lack of risk assessment as seen in the *India-Agricultural Products* case.

A converse and interesting point is that "[n]o process exists in the SPS Agreement for challenging the adoption of SPS measures that are less protective of human, animal, or plant life and health than international standards" (Kennedy 2000, 87).

The significant issue is the lack of knowledge regarding diseases emerging in Arctic and Antarctic resources. There is a plethora of new scientific information highlighting the problem of increased disease transmission in fragile environments, lacking in resilience due to their geographically and climatically induced isolation. Further, many exportation guidelines in force at check points such as abattoirs, may not take into consideration the increased susceptibility of a naive environment. That is, how do we know the level of resilience or the level of disease presence allowable for endemic areas? Perhaps the best approach is to have a zero risk approach, that is, all risk assessments for export to polar regions or export from polar regions have a zero risk standard.

Article 2.3 will be considered by the *Mexico-Avocados* case, the complaint filed regarding arbitrary or unjustifiable discrimination being on the issue as "between Costa Rica's own territory and the territory of Mexico".[20]

b Mexican avocados case

On 8 March 2017, a request for consultation was filed with the DSB for alleged violations of Article 11.1[21] of the SPS Agreement for an alleged violation. The claim has been made against measures imposed by Costa Rica in relation to the importation of Mexican avocados. Violations are alleged against Articles 2.1, 2.2, 2.3, 3.1, 5.1, 5.2, 5.3, 5.4, 5.5, 5.6, 5.7, 5.8, 6.1, 6.2, 7, 8, and paragraphs 2, 5 and 6 of Annex B and paragraph 1 of Annex C to the SPS Agreement as well as Articles I:1, III:4, X and XI of the GATT 1994.

The initial request for consultations (13 March 2007) listed that measures (including a law, a regulation, resolution, and pest risk analysis) adopted by Costa Rica on the restrictions or prohibition of the importation of fresh avocados from Mexico were in violation of the SPS Agreement, mentioning initially, the failure to adapt such measures to regional conditions, including those areas of disease- and pest-free or reduced prevalence (Article 6) and the requirement of the SPS Agreement to ensure an opportunity for exporting Members to make a claim under this Article.[22] Upon failure to settle the dispute, a request for panel establishment to resolve the dispute was made on 22 November 2018.

The case revolves on pest risk analysis for Avocado sunblotch viroid (ASBVd) and took issue with an extensive number of the SPS provisions, alleging violation based on SPS measures involving regulations and pest risk assessments. Mexico listed issue with Articles 1.1, 2.1, 2.2, 2.3, 3.1, 3.3, 5.1 (where the transmission via importation does not consider techniques developed by the International Plant Protection

Convention), 5.2, 5.3, 5.5, 5.6 and 6.1. Further, it listed violations of the GATT 1994 Articles III:4 and XI:1.[23] The panel report for this case is due to come out before the end of 2020 and will be both an extensive discussion of the SPS provisions and speak to current relevant application at a time when biosecurity around trade is increasingly in the international view.

3.3.7 *Article 2.4: Understanding the exception under GATT Article XX (b)*

Article XX(b) was the original provision for food safety (Kennedy 2000, 83). However, as Kennedy says, "No process exists in the SPS Agreement for challenging the adoption of SPS measures that are *less* protective of human, animal, or plant life and health than international standards." (Kennedy 2000, 87, emphasis added). Article XX(b) GATT 1994 formed the basis of the later-articulated SPS Agreement[24], its preamble now stating its connection; "Desiring therefore to elaborate rules for the application of the provisions of GATT 1994 which relate to the use of sanitary or phytosanitary measures, in particular the provisions of Article XX(b) (1)". The effect of this Article, and the presumed consistency with the GATT 1994, has been under discussion, particularly given the duality of consistency provided by this Article and Article 3.2 where consistency with GATT 1994 is also mentioned (Gruszczynski 2010, 94–96).[25]

Under Article 2.4, measures conforming with the SPS Agreement are *presumed* consistent with the GATT 1994; possibly providing a non-rebuttable presumption (Gruszczynski 2010, 94). This works to ensure that the provisions of the SPS are not cumulative and rather independently applicable, depending on the circumstances involved.[26] Article 3.2, mentioned in the GATT 1994, establishes a rebuttable "presumption of consistency with the SPS Agreement for those measures which conform to international standards" where the Article specifies that "a measure conforming to international standard is deemed to be necessary to protect human, animal, or plant life or health and presumed to be consistent with the relevant provisions of the SPS Agreement and of GATT 1994" (Gruszczynski 2010, 94). The two Articles cannot be read the same, as it would deprive Article 3.2 of full meaning (ibid., 95).

At the very least, it may be agreed that compatibility with the SPS Agreement and GATT 1994 "has to be regarded as necessary since the necessity test constitutes one of the requirements under both agreements" (Gruszczynski 2010, 95).

3.4 Article 5: Risk assessment, control and inspection

**Assessment of risk and determination of the appropriate
level of sanitary or phytosanitary protection**

1 Members shall ensure that their sanitary or phytosanitary measures are based on an assessment, as appropriate to the circumstances, of the risks to human, animal or plant life or health, taking into account risk assessment techniques developed by the relevant international organizations.

2 In the assessment of risks, Members shall take into account available scientific evidence; relevant processes and production methods; relevant inspection, sampling and testing methods; prevalence of specific diseases or pests; existence of pest- or disease- free areas; relevant ecological and environmental conditions; and quarantine or other treatment.

3 In assessing the risk to animal or plant life or health and determining the measure to be applied for achieving the appropriate level of sanitary or phytosanitary protection from such risk, Members shall take into account as relevant economic factors: the potential damage in terms of loss of production or sales in the event of the entry, establishment or spread of a pest or disease; the costs of control or eradication in the territory of the importing Member; and the relative cost-effectiveness of alternative approaches to limiting risks.

4 Members should, when determining the appropriate level of sanitary or phytosanitary protection, take into account the objective of minimising negative trade effects.

5 With the objective of achieving consistency in the application of the concept of appropriate level of sanitary or phytosanitary protection against risks to human life or health, or to animal and plant life or health, each Member shall avoid arbitrary or unjustifiable distinctions in the levels it considers to be appropriate in different situations, if such distinctions result in discrimination or a disguised restriction on international trade. Members shall cooperate in the Committee, in accordance with paragraphs 1, 2 and 3 of Article 12, to develop guidelines to further the practical implementation of this provision. In developing the guidelines, the Committee shall take into account all relevant factors, including the exceptional character of human health risks to which people voluntarily expose themselves.

6 Without prejudice to paragraph 2 of Article 3, when establishing or maintaining sanitary or phytosanitary measures to achieve the appropriate level of sanitary or phytosanitary protection, Members

shall ensure that such measures are not more trade-restrictive than required to achieve their appropriate level of sanitary or phytosanitary protection, taking into account technical and economic feasibility.

7 In cases where relevant scientific evidence is insufficient, a Member may provisionally adopt sanitary or phytosanitary measures on the basis of available pertinent information, including that from the relevant international organisations as well as from sanitary or phytosanitary measures applied by other Members. In such circumstances, Members shall seek to obtain the additional information necessary for a more objective assessment of risk and review the sanitary or phytosanitary measure accordingly within a reasonable period of time.

8 When a Member has reason to believe that a specific sanitary or phytosanitary measure introduced or maintained by another Member is constraining, or has the potential to constrain, its exports and the measure is not based on the relevant international standards, guidelines or recommendations, or such standards, guidelines or recommendations do not exist, an explanation of the reasons for such sanitary or phytosanitary measure may be requested and shall be provided by the Member maintaining the measure.

Article 5 derives its meaning and context in part from Article 2 (*EC-Hormones*, para 180). As already noted, a violation of Articles 5.1 or 5.2 may lead to a violation of Article 2.2 and a violation of Article 5.7 does lead to a violation of Article 2.2. This is because an "importing Member's assessment of the SPS characteristics of the relevant areas may, in certain cases, be conducted as part of a Member's risk assessment pursuant to Articles 5.1 through 5.3." (*Russia-Pigs*, AB, para 5.71).

3.4.1 Article 5.1

A violation of Article 5.1 is inconsistent with Article 2.2 because the absence of risk assessment means a measure is not based on scientific evidence (*Australia-Salmon*, AB, para 138). "Article 2.2 informs Article 5.1: the elements that define the basic obligation set out in Article 2.2 impart meaning to Article 5.1" (*Australia-Apples,* AB, para 339). This does not leave much scope for a nation of the littoral Arctic or those responsible for the custodianship of the Antarctic to constrain importation of goods on the basis of, for example, supposition or initial anecdotal evidence. In the case of preserving endemic polar regions, a shared burden by both exporting and importing Members may be more effective: exporting nations be required to certify a product for export at zero-disease presence, while importing polar zones are responsible for monitoring possible vectors making incursions into higher latitudes. As such, the burden for trading with an Arctic nation is shared and for the purpose of protecting endemic polar environments. In this sense, there must necessarily be a precautionary approach to the risks, which may entail an overestimation of those risks.

The *Australia-Apples* panel found that an overestimation of the risks was not based on scientific evidence (para 222). This approach was found consistent with other decisions of the Appellate Body (*EC-Hormones*, AB, para 193; *Japan-Agricultural Products II*, AB, para 84;[27] *Japan-Apples*, AB, para 162[28]), where there needed to be an objective relationship among the SPS measures, risk assessment and the scientific evidence. Such overestimation makes an SPS measure invalid which is problematic for the polar regions, unless this article can be considered better with Article 6.

Further to controlling any overestimation, in *Australia-Salmon* (para 123, FN 13), it was noted that a risk assessment must address the probability or likelihood of pathogenic entry, establishment or spread, (cited in *Japan-Agricultural Products*, AB, para 78). It does not seem that the measure need relate to a specific pathogen. This may be an oversight given that pathogen have particular pathogenesis and pose specific risks to specific species. Constraining measures based on knowledge of a pathogen is another way of ensuring proper risk assessment, and also the possibility for use of the precautionary principle where such knowledge is missing, as argued by Japan in *Japan-Agricultural Products* (AB, para 81).

It is Annex A of the SPS Agreement, paragraph 4, that defines risk assessment as "[t]he evaluation of the likelihood of entry, establishment or spread of a pest or disease within the territory of an importing Member according to the sanitary or phytosanitary measures which might be applied, and of the associated potential biological and economic consequences" and so must do three things:

1 Identify diseases whose entry, establishment of spread is sought to be prevented;
2 Likelihood of entry, establishment or spread;
3 Likelihood of entry, establishment or spread given the SPS measure (*Australia-Salmon* cited in *Japan-Apples*, AB, para 196).

This series of tests is problematic for the Arctic and Antarctic when infiltration of and transmission of new disease is so dependent on dynamic factors. A risk assessment needs to be specific to the case, meaning the product at issue (*Japan-Apples,* AB, paras 199–216), although in *Japan-Apples* the case did not address whether the risk assessment "should be evaluated solely against the scientific evidence *available at the time of* the risk assessment, to the exclusion of subsequent information" (AB, para 215, emphasis added). Hosts of disease or vectors need to be considered only where they relate specifically to the SPS measure in issue, that is, the harm concerned, the precise agent that may cause the harm and the specific pathway of harm or contamination (*Japan-Apples,* AB, paras 202 and 204). Risk assessments may be organised along the "lines of the disease or pest at issue, or of the commodity to be imported" (*Japan-Apples* AB, para 204). Deficiency of scientific evidence available at the time of the risk assessment as yet has not been grounds for deferring to the precautionary principle (it failed in *Japan-Apples*, see AB report para 214–215), yet the use of the precautionary principle is the better approach for considering risk-averse trade, particularly in endemic zones. At present, deference to unknown science is not considered legitimate within the risk assessment framework within the context of Article 5. This is because the act of performing a risk assessment presupposes that there is sufficient evidence to conduct such an assessment (*Australia-Apples,* AB, para 241). However, *EC-Hormones* allowed Members to respond to risk assessments by adopting stricter or more precautionary measures (Gruszczynski 2010, 169).

In 2010, the Appellate Body in *Australia-Apples* (another case involving fire blight) referred to *US/Canada-Continued Suspension*[29] and concurred that a panel only has the responsibility to determine whether a risk assessment is supported by "coherent reasoning and respectable scientific evidence and is, in this sense, objectively justifiable", specifically whether the scientific basis is a "respected and qualified source" with the "necessary scientific and methodological rigour [sic] to be considered reputable science" (*US/Canada-Continued Suspension,* AB, paras 590–591, cited *Australia-Apples,* AB, paras 213–214). The panel in assessing the risk assessment may examine the "underlying scientific basis and scrutiny of the reasoning of the risk assessor based upon such underlying science" (*Australia-Apples,* AB, para 215). Thus, in *Australia–Apples,* the Appellate Body summarised the requirements of the panel in assessing a risk assessors assessment as twofold: "(i) a determination that the scientific basis of the risk assessment comes from a respected and qualified source and can accordingly be considered "legitimate science" according to the standards of the relevant scientific community; and (ii) a determination that the reasoning of the risk assessor is objective and coherent and that, therefore, its conclusions find sufficient support in the underlying scientific basis" (*Australia-Apples,* AB, para 220).

A panel is not the primary organ for scientific research and assessments (*EC-Hormones,* AB, para 117) and cannot substitute its own reasoning for that of a risk assessor (*US/Canada-Continued Suspension,* AB, para 590). Assessing the latter includes assessing intermediate conclusions or reasoning (*Australia-Apples,* AB, para 229): scrutiny of the source of the evidence differs from scrutiny of the risk assessor's reasoning (*Australia-Apples,* AB, para 225). This includes that, where an expert is used, the panel needs to have transparency as to *how* the risk assessor was used, not simply that one was used (*Australia-Apples,* AB, para 247).

3.4.2 Article 5.2

Article 5.2 mandates a number of factors to be considered in the assessment of risk. The first four of these relate to the science around the disease and agent of disease and method of detection for the disease: available scientific evidence; relevant processes and production methods; relevant inspection, sampling and testing methods; and prevalence of specific diseases or pests. The last three factors relate broadly to factors which may impact upon the impact of the disease or potential impact of the disease: existence of pest- or disease-free areas; relevant ecological and environmental conditions; and quarantine or other treatment. The relationship between these factors – all seven of them – is certain. In *Australia-Apples,* it was found that Australia's risk assessment did not take into account the pathogen's viability and period of emergence which are specific aspects of the agent of disease. Yet in the same sentence, "the impact of parasitism…climatic conditions, and mode of trade" were not considered sufficiently to bring the risk assessment into question (AB, para 256; PR, para. 7.871). As far as the polar regions are concerned, this case, on this Article, is significant. It places in relationship factors that cover aspects of emerging disease whilst allowing scope for considering further impacts of climate and mode of trade. Where there is no available scientific evidence, recourse to an expert may be the best option to assess risk, but the use of any expert by a Member must still set out reasonable conclusions, including intermediate conclusions (*Australia-Apples,* AB, para 234). Use of an expert must satisfy requirements under Articles 5.1 and 5.2, otherwise recourse to a provisional measure under Article 5.7 might be a better option (*Australia-Apples*, AB, paras 237–238).

3.4.3 Article 5.3

Article 5.3 furthers the factors to be taken into account from Article 5.2 where a risk assessment is conducted; it must also take economic factors: economic costs due to disease entry and spread; the costs of control or eradication; and the relative cost-effectiveness of alternative approaches to limiting risks. Consideration of such factors does not direct a course of action (*Russia-Pigs (EU)*, PR, para 7.767) and uncertainty does not justify departure from the requirements (*Australia-Salmon*, AB), which includes any precautionary approach not justifying any departure. This applies for Article 5.1 also. Article 5.3, read as part of Articles 5.1 and 5.2, stands separate from the requirements for provisions measures under Article 5.7.

3.4.4 Article 5.4

Article 5.4 serves as the counterpoint for the Article, protecting the interests of trade in determination of an ALOP, though it does so without qualification or any stringent considerations; is not an obligation (*EC-Hormones (Canada)*,[30] PR, para 8.169; *EC-Hormones (US)*, PR, para 8.166[31]), but may be considered a specific application of a measure applied to the extent necessary to protect life or health without arbitrary or unjustifiable discrimination (*EC-Hormones (US)*, PR, para 8.99; and *EC-Hormones (Canada)*, PR, para 8.96). So, the full effect of this article may be only that a risk assessment needs to have a consideration of proportion to trade access, mentioned in a risk assessment, and that is all.

3.4.5 Article 5.5

Reference in Article 5.5 to "arbitrary or unjustifiable", and "discrimination or a disguised restriction on international trade" may follow the same delineations as used elsewhere in the SPS Agreement, applied in this case to the levels of protection provided by SPS measures. The phrase in the first sentence of Article 5.5 specifically states, "shall avoid arbitrary or unjustifiable distinctions in the levels it considers to be appropriate *in different situations...*" (emphasis added). This addition to the otherwise familiar expressions is important. There is no clarification for what *in different situations* means, though may grant greater protection measures in unique situations of the polar regions which include consideration for the higher susceptibility (lower resilience due to a lack of exposure) of indigenous health and endemic species. In furtherance of identifying a practical implementation, the SPS Committee is to take into account relevant factors including, strangely "the exceptional character of human health risks to which people voluntarily expose themselves". This article may be another specification of the obligation of only applying a measure to the extent necessary to protect life and health without being arbitrary or unjustifiably discriminatory under Articles 2.2 and 2.3, specifically in relation to applying an ALOP (*EC-Hormones* (*US*), PR, para 8.99; and *EC-Hormones* (*Canada*), PR, para 8.96).

Three elements need to be satisfied for an Article 5.5 inconsistency: (i) ALOP's must be consistent (*EC-Hormones*, AB, paras 213) and not generic across potentially comparable situations (*Australia-Apples*, PR, paras 7.970–7.971); (ii) ALOPs applied with arbitrary or unjustifiable differences across different situations (*EC-Hormones*, AB, para 214) which includes across differing levels of sanitary protection as long as they are comparable, that is, they present a common element/s sufficient to render them rationally comparable (*EC-Hormones*, AB, para 217); and (iii) the arbitrary or unjustifiable differences result in discrimination or a disguised restriction of international trade, given interpretation under the *Vienna Convention of the Law on Treaties* that the ordinary interpretation be used, that is, the measure not "capricious, unpredictable, inconsistent" (*US-Poultry* (*China*), PR, para 7.259)[32] and that, in line with the reading within Article 2.3, the chapeau of GATT Article XX is to be followed examining the measure in light of its cause, rationale and objectives (*US-Poultry* (*China*), PR, paras 7.260–7.261).

As these three are cumulative (*EC-Hormones,* AB, para 215), and it is probable that situations in the high latitudes "are totally different from one another, they would not be rationally comparable and the differences in levels of protection cannot be examined for arbitrariness" (*EC-Hormones*, AB, para 217). Thus, the article at this stage of WTO jurisprudence does not pose as a great concern for the polar regions. As a secondary fail-safe, the second element applies only where there is no need for "both the disease and the biological and economic consequences to be the same or similar" (*Australia-Salmon*, AB, para 146), thus where only the disease is comparable is sufficient to adjudge an inconsistency, giving more scope to protecting endemic areas.

3.4.6 Article 5.6

Article 5.6 continues the inclusion of the preferential trade liberality of the WTO environment and requires consideration that levels of protection are "not more trade-restrictive than required...taking into account technical and economic feasibility". Three conditions must be satisfied: that another measure (i) is reasonably available taking into account technical and economic feasibility; (ii) achieves the importing Member's appropriate level of sanitary or phytosanitary protection; and (iii) is significantly less restrictive to trade than the SPS measure(s) at issue in the dispute (*Australia-Apples,* AB, paras 328 and 360; *Australia-Salmon,* AB, para 194; *Japan-Agricultural Products II,* AB, para. 95).

The primary consideration is whether there is a measure that is less restrictive whilst achieving the same outcome, that is the same ALOP as stated by the Member issuing the restrictions. In order to do this, there needs to be "sufficient undisputed facts on the Panel record to... determine what level of protection would be achieved" and whether that amounted to the ALOP required (*Australia-Apples,* AB, para 386).

This is significant. Where a Member provides an acceptable level of risk that is low but not zero, this allows movement of the safety net (*Australia-Apples,* AB, para 360). In the *Australia-Apples* case, Australia was prevented from refusing importation to New Zealand Apples on the basis of a zero risk threshold because their policy did not itself specify the need for a zero risk threshold, rather it had one that reduced the threat to minimal. In the case of the poles, a zero risk policy ought to be adopted to avoid a similar contention.

Assessing the level of risk associated with an SPS measure or other alternatives determines consistency with this provision and "is a question of legal characterization...Answering this question is not a task that can be delegated to scientific experts" (*Australia-Apples*, PR, para 384)[33]. Assessment requires legal analysis comparing the implemented measure and any alternative measure (*Australia-Apples,* AB, para 385), including the overall risk associated with the alternative measure proposed, that is, the "risk of entry, establishment and spread ... as well as the associated potential biological and economic consequences" (*Australia-Apples,* AB, para 402). Such assessment, however, must be careful not to fall into *de novo* review (*Australia-Apples,* AB, para 351).

Finally, Articles 5.6 and 2.2 need to be read together (*India-Agricultural Products*, PR, para 7.614; Panel Report, *Russia-Pigs* (*EU*), paras 7.841–7.842), as the same relationship between Articles 5.2 and 2.2 (*Australia-Apples,* AB, para 339).

3.4.7 Article 5.7

Article 5.7 has already been discussed above in its relationship with Article 2.2. Generally, Article 5 shares a complicated relationship with Article 2.2, their legal validity and satisfaction running together (*Japan-Agricultural Products II*). Where a measure is shown to be consistent with Article 5.7, it will be found to have consistency with Article 2.2 (*Japan-Agricultural Products II*). Where there is insufficient scientific evidence to perform a risk assessment, "a WTO Member may take a provisional SPS measure on the basis provided in Article 5.7, but that Member must meet the obligations set out in that provision" (*US/Canada-Continued Suspension*, AB, para 674). As regards the Arctic and Antarctic, the interpretation given to the place of Article 5.7 in relation to Article 2.2 is important: Article 5.7 is a qualification or exemption to Article 2.2 (*Japan-Agricultural Products II*, AB, para. 80) covering those instances not covered by Article 2.2. A qualified exemption exists where there is insufficient scientific evidence and a provisional measure is adopted, not reading the provision too broadly to render the article meaningless (*Japan-Agricultural Products II*, AB, para 80). Four requirements that must be satisfied in order to adopt and maintain a provisional measure:

1 Insufficient relevant scientific evidence;
2 Measure adopted is on the basis of available pertinent information;
3 Member seeks to obtain the additional information necessary for a more objective assessment of risk; and
4 Member reviews the measure within a reasonable period of time" (*Japan-Apples,* AB, para 176 referring to *Japan-Agricultural Products II*, AB, para 89).

Notions of relevance and insufficiency (in the first requirement) need to be coherent and read in the context of Article 5, specifically Article 5.1: relevant scientific evidence is insufficient if the body of "available scientific evidence does not allow, in quantitative or qualitative terms, the performance of an adequate" risk assessment under Article 5.1 (*Japan-Agricultural Products II*, AB, para 179). The evidence can be general or specific, and may be cumulative over years (as it was in *Japan-Agricultural Products II*, that the risk of fire blight transmission through mature symptomless apples was negligible, para 180).

Given the nature of a provisional measure, Article 5.7 may reflect use of the precautionary principle within the frame of this provision (*EC-Hormones,* AB, paras 123–124; *EC-Marketing of Biotech Products*, PR, para 7.87[34] Gruszczynski 2010, 215). In particular, there is no definitive understanding as to the influence of "pertinent information...the development status of a Member, and domestic regulatory priorities in the assessment of the obligations to seek to obtain additional information…as well as the treatment of situations that are characterized by low certainty and low consensus when calculating a reasonable period of time" (ibid., 216). Better understanding the pathogen-host-environment relationship, the pathogen and relevant pathogenesis, may also satisfy the requirement for a *rational relationship between the measure and the risk assessment* under *EC-Hormones* standard.

3.4.8 Article 5.8

When Member believes measure is or will be constraining to exports and not based on international standards (even where they do not exist), the exporter can request an explanation of the reasons for the restriction. This Article potentially bears an undue burden on polar regions, which adopt a high level of protection based on insufficient scientific evidence because such environments are naïve. It points to the overwhelming need for a provision to be negotiated for preferential trade barriers in polar environments where warming climate and increased trade may pose hazards as yet unknown. A potential reason may be the inherent value of the polar regions and the emerging evidence of increased spread, transmission, and mortality to polar species, which have no immunity to temperate region pathogens.

RETURNING TO STANDARD-SETTING FOR THE ENDEMIC POLES

3.5 A principled approach to technical trade barriers: Using a precautionary approach

Given the priority advocated here for the use of Article 6 in adjusting any standards set internationally for the polar regions, the necessary corollary is the admission that scientific evidence of the changing nature of transmission and transmissibility of disease in these changing regions is, as yet, underdeveloped. As such, regard to the precautionary principle and its greater use in arguments for risk assessment under Article 5 may be increasingly seen.

The precautionary principle has found to have a role in understanding Articles 2.2, 3.3, 5.1 and 5.7 (Gruszczynski 2010, 213–214). Article 5.7 is arguably the clearest embodiment of the principle, permitting "regulatory action even without the existence of conclusive scientific evidence as to the nature of hazard and the extent of potential risk…

[but] presupposes the provisional character of precautionary measures by mandating their review once new scientific information becomes available" (Gruszczynski 2010, 215). Given that within Article 5.7, it makes no reference to international trade and non-discrimination, this seems to give wider scope to regulators for using the precautionary principle (ibid.). The precautionary principle was argued to be used in place of definitive scientific knowledge in *Japan-Agricultural Products* being argued that the curtailing of the relevance of the precautionary principle seemed unduly harsh (AB, para 81).

EC-Hormones linked the precautionary principle with the SPS Agreement, stating that the principle could be used to assess the sufficiency of scientific evidence underscoring a measure, given "representative governments commonly act from perspectives of prudence and precaution where risks of irreversible, e.g. life terminating, damage to human health are concerned" (AB, para 124). There is discernment to determine those occasions where an irreversible risk is grave enough, given as effects of pathogens, once introduced to an unexposed system may not be reversed, though in this sense, this Article may work to the advantage of naïve ecosystems. There is no mention of *proportion* in this sentence, that is, where a low proportion of the population/environment is threatened, and so ought not to be included in an assessment of risk to human health. Although *EC-Hormones* has not clarified the position of the precautionary principle in the SPS jurisprudence, specifically since "the EC failed to explain how...the precautionary principle would affect the specific requirements provided in the SPS Agreement" (Gruszczynski 2010, 167).

The precautionary approach is less about managing risks than managing potential risks, particularly *environmental risks* as identified under the "1992 Rio Declaration which provided that 'where there are threats of serious or irreversible damage, lack of full scientific certainty shall not be used as a reason for postponing cost-effective measures to prevent environmental degradation' (Gruszczynski 2010, 159).[35] There are many formulations of the precautionary principle, all with slight modifications from the Rio Declaration. Some require a cost-benefit analysis, others a certainty of no-harm (for a good discussion, see Gruszczynski 2010, 162). In the context of trade in the polar regions, it is argued that where the appropriate level of risk is zero and where scientific evidence falls short of sufficiency (and likely to remain so given the dynamic situation), its use is warranted. Just how it is used is another question where "the heterogeneity of the formulations of the principle" may be used differently in country submissions

(Gruszczynski 2010, 166). It has been considered problematic to apply the precautionary principle or approach to the SPS Agreement:

> First, this requires prior determination of the status of the principle (that is, whether it can be qualified as a rule of customary international law or general principle of international law). Second, if the answer is positive, one has to determine to what extent and how this rule may have an impact on the disciplines of the Agreement. (Gruszczynski 2010, 166)

This conjecture of difficulty is based on the application of a precautionary principle hithertofore discussed in the international community and, as yet, not agreed upon (either formulation or application). However, the inclusion of a precautionary principle within the SPS Agreement neither has to harken back to the academic discussion, nor has to be dispelled because its existence as custom is not settled. It may be considered in its own merit; that is, in its own formulation (whether indirect or direct application as discussed in *EC-Hormones*, Gruszczynski 2010, 167).

In relation to the SPS Agreement, the precautionary principle through its application in cases where there is insufficiency of scientific evidence finds a place in provision measures allowed under Article 5.7, its application lying somewhere between "incremental advances of science on one side and a paradigm shift on the other" (Gruszczynski 2010, 202). This is regardless of international standards which "do not create any legal presumption of sufficiency for the purpose of Article 5.7" (ibid., 203).

There remains a question as to whether the regimes for risk assessment laid out in the SPS Agreement, actually propose two separate regimes: one where there is sufficiency of scientific evidence under Articles 2.2 and 5.1 and one using the precautionary principle upon insufficiency of scientific evidence under Article 5.7 (Gruszczynski 2010, 217). Whether a division such as this would be beneficial to better safeguarding the endemic populations and naive ecosystems of the Arctic and Antarctic is uncertain: the primary issue in these regions, as far as the SPS Agreement is concerned, is deciphering the application of Article 6 as a paramount concern and then the relationship between Article 5.7 and Article 6, taking it as given that there will be, at least in the immediate future, an insufficiency of scientific evidence.

Finally, whilst use of the precautionary principle through Article 5.7 may give wider latitude to governments for applying higher standards of protection, the regions of the poles to be sufficiently safeguarded need a coordinated, regional approach. It bears little hope if one Arctic littoral nation applies strict standards and the next much lower standards because where borders are not recognised by migrating strains of virus or bacteria newly resilient to the colder climate or adverse to being transported on the skin of migrating seals or penguin, then higher levels of protection in only one place will not prove sufficient.

3.6 Returning to standard setting under the SPS Agreement

Coming full circle, the application of the SPS Agreement very much hinges on the standards recognised under the SPS Agreement. This puts the OIE in the driver's seat when it comes to animals and animal products. As stated by the Appellate Body in *India-Agricultural Products*, "Annex A(3)(b) to the SPS Agreement recognizes the OIE as the relevant standard-setting body for SPS measures relating to animal health and zoonoses" (para 4.14). The OIE, as the body with the highest relevance to issues of trade in animals and animal products into and out of the Arctic/Antarctic, has two standard types; "(i) health standards on trade in animals and their products...and (ii) biological standards on diagnostic techniques...included in the Terrestrial Animal Health Code...and the Aquatic Animal Health Code" (Gruszczynski 2010, 84).

The OIE has permanent observer status with the SPS Committee and "Representatives of the OIE are invited to attend meetings of the SPS Committee and to participate, without voting rights, in deliberations on items on the agenda in which the OIE has an interest, with the exception of meetings limited to WTO Members" (ibid.). The role of the OIE in relation to curbing disease spread was enunciated in the same case:

> 4.15. Members of the OIE annually adopt the OIE Terrestrial Animal Health Code (OIE Code), the aim of which is to set international standards for the improvement of terrestrial animal health and welfare and veterinary public health worldwide, including through standards for safe international trade in terrestrial animals, including mammals, birds, and bees, and their products. The OIE Code contains recommendations that are based on the most up-to-date scientific information and available techniques, and that are designed to prevent specific diseases from being introduced into the importing country, taking into account the nature of the commodity and the animal health status of the exporting

country. The recommendations in the OIE Code, when correctly applied, provide for safe international trade in animals and animal products while avoiding unjustified sanitary barriers to trade. ...
4.16. The OIE Code contains numerous substantive provisions and recommendations grouped into two volumes. Volume I comprises general provisions that concern horizontal standards applicable to a wide range of species, production sectors, and diseases. Volume II contains recommendations applicable to OIE-listed diseases and other diseases of importance to international trade. This volume sets out the standards that apply in respect of specific diseases, including recommendations regarding disease surveillance and zoning and compartmentalisation. (*Japan-Agricultural Products II,* AB)

Under Article 3, it has been held that there are three options available to Members, "a Member may conform to international standards, only base its measures on such standards, or deviate from them completely. Each of these situations brings its own specific legal consequences" (Gruszczynski 2010, 105). In the first instance, conformity is presumed and the presumption is broad, in the second instance, the evidentiary basis is made easier by enabling reliance on science that formed the basis of a standard (ibid., 105–106). However, where international standards fail to consider regional endemism, only the third option is truly available. Under this option, there needs to be a risk assessment and scientific sufficiency as required under Article 5 (ibid.).

3.7 Article 3: Using stricter protocols – The problems with scientific evidence, technical knowledge and non-equivalence

Harmonisation

1 To harmonise sanitary and phytosanitary measures on as wide a basis as possible, Members shall base their sanitary or phytosanitary measures on international standards, guidelines or recommendations, where they exist, except as otherwise provided for in this Agreement, and in particular in paragraph 3.
2 Sanitary or phytosanitary measures which conform to international standards, guidelines or recommendations shall be deemed to be necessary to protect human, animal or plant life or health, and presumed to be consistent with the relevant provisions of this Agreement and of GATT 1994.

3 Members may introduce or maintain sanitary or phytosanitary measures which result in a higher level of sanitary or phytosanitary protection than would be achieved by measures based on the relevant international standards, guidelines or recommendations, if there is a scientific justification, or as a consequence of the level of sanitary or phytosanitary protection, a Member determines to be appropriate in accordance with the relevant provisions of paragraphs 1 through 8 of Article 5. Notwithstanding the above, all measures which result in a level of sanitary or phytosanitary protection different from that which would be achieved by measures based on international standards, guidelines or recommendations shall not be inconsistent with any other provision of this Agreement.

4 Members shall play a full part, within the limits of their resources, in the relevant international organisations and their subsidiary bodies, in particular, the Codex Alimentarius Commission, the International Office of Epizootics, and the international and regional organisations operating within the framework of the International Plant Protection Convention, to promote within these organisations the development and periodic review of standards, guidelines and recommendations with respect to all aspects of sanitary and phytosanitary measures.

5 The Committee on Sanitary and Phytosanitary Measures provided for in paragraphs 1 and 4 of Article 12 (referred to in this Agreement as the "Committee") shall develop a procedure to monitor the process of international harmonisation and coordinate efforts in this regard with the relevant international organisations.

Article 3 appears to be a step-wise approach to bringing national standards in line with international standards for the protection of human, animal, or plant life or health. Subarticle 1 is the definitive statement. Subarticle 2 makes a presumption in favour of international standards being to protect human, animal, or plant life or health. This opens the door to future standards developed in favour of the polar regions being justifiable as the foundation for SPS measures. Subarticle 3 allows stricter Member control, beneficial for protection of endemic environments where there is scientific justification. Subarticle 4 mandates the contribution of Members to the relevant international bodies responsible for developing standards and guidelines and subarticle 5 stipulates the Committee referred in Article 12 as monitoring body.

Subarticles 3.1, 3.2 and 3.3 cover different types of situations: the first has no presumption of conformity though presumably a presumption of non-contradiction with international standards; the second has a presumption of conformity with international standards (*EC-Hormones* (*Canada*), PR, para 8.75; *EC-Hormones* (*US*), para 8.72), the third recognises the "autonomous right of a Member to establish such higher level of protection" (*EC-Hormones*, AB, para 104). Where Members' levels of trade restriction are not to be "more trade restrictive than required to achieve the appropriate level of protection" (Kennedy 2000, 87), it is subarticle 3.2 that carries the presumption of being in line with the GATT 1994 (*US/Canada-Continued Suspension*, AB, para 694), in particular, GATT 1994 Article XX.

The interesting part of Article 3 is subarticle 3. The footnote in the original to this article specifies "there is a scientific justification if, on the basis of an examination and evaluation of available scientific information in conformity with the relevant provisions of this Agreement, a Member determines that the relevant international standards, guidelines or recommendations are not sufficient to achieve its appropriate level of sanitary or phytosanitary protection". This also has been determined to lead back to satisfying the requirements of Article 5 and paragraph 4 of Annex A of the SPS Agreement (*EC-Hormones*, AB, paras 173, 175, and 176). Indeed inconsistency with Article 5.1 and Articles 2.2, 2.3, 5.6 and 6.1 may be a further ground for a violation of Article 3.3 (*US-Animals*, PR, para 7.721)[36].

Article 3 should not be underestimated in relation to the polar regions. In naïve environments where there is unknown hosts, vectors, transmission and risk and thus high probability that risk assessments cannot be based on available and relevant scientific evidence, the use of guidelines will be first port-of-call. What these guidelines are and who determines them is significant. The exclusion of regional bodies from the international sphere is also significant where regional bodies involved in the polar regions will have relevant scientific studies and, if not, will understand the limitations. And finally, where there are no guidelines, deference to the precautionary principle may contend with other agreements such as the Technical Barriers to Trade (TBT) Agreement, which "encourages members to base their measures on international standards as a means to facilitate trade".[37] Reference here to international standards, however, may also draw back to those international standards as mentioned in Article 3.2.

3.7.1 Article 3.2

Article 3.2, mentioned in the GATT 1994, establishes a rebuttable "presumption of consistency with the SPS Agreement for those measures which conform to international standards" where the Article specifies that "a measure conforming to international standard is deemed to be necessary to protect human, animal, or plant life or health and presumed to be consistent with the relevant provisions of the SPS Agreement and of GATT 1994" (Gruszczynski 2010, 94). Leaving to one side the delineations and proofs of "deemed" and "presumed", a rebuttable presumption in Article 3.2 is necessary in order to accommodate those situations where insufficient scientific evidence makes a measure appropriate in the short term, but inappropriate once new evidence comes to light, but the measure has not been altered immediately (ibid., 95). In other words, it allows accommodation where the precautionary principle is, at least initially, used. Following from this, another reading may simply see that international standards are a good and measured path to adopting protocols that are protective, particularly in the case where the international body has better evidence on a particular pathogen or its pathogenesis than a nation might. Conformity with that standard is deemed necessary for protective purposes, that is, it cannot be held to be over-protective. However, this does not mean that it creates binding norms of international standards, contrary to the argument of Gruszczynski (2010, 95).

To determine whether subarticle 3.2 has been justifiably used, "a panel must engage in a comparative assessment between the challenged measure and that international standard...the international standard serves as the benchmark against which a Member's compliance under Article 3 is to be assessed" (*India-Agricultural Products*, AB, para 5.79)[38]. This idea of comparison has been used in *US-Animals* (PR, para 7.222) and may require the evaluation of actions of both the importer and exporter (*Russia-Pigs (EU)*, PR, para 7.865).

However, there is no real basis for comparison because the standards set by international bodies are not equivalent to norms; the standards are not obligatory (*EC-Hormones*, AB, para 165). If standards impose non-obligations, then in polar regions, there may be an issue where polar-based Members impose restrictions based on initial scientific research. The use of the precautionary approach may provide a remedy. The decision in *India-Agricultural Products* could be applied, where it was considered that the standards, whilst not obligatory, could also not be contradicted (PR, para 7.269). The question then becomes what constitutes a contradiction. Perhaps measures that are different for different products or are "conditional on the exporting Member undertaking particular actions...may introduce temporal considerations or may require additional action" would not be contradictory (*Russia-Pigs (EU)*, PR, para 7.259). Where measures are put in place to protect against a number of diseases, even where standards do not exist for the whole number but only one, for example, that standard may still be applied to the measure at issue (*Australia-Salmon*, PR, para 8.46). This is perhaps a little confusing. It may be better, where the standard applicable to one disease for a particular species may apply to the measure *with regard to that particular disease in that particular species*. Indeed, the SPS Agreement will run afoul of its purpose if the very specific nature of disease, host, and transmission is not acknowledged.

3.7.2 Article 3.3

The precautionary principle is reflected in subarticle 3.3 (*EC-Hormones*, AB, para 124). A measure that is based on an international standard does not need to conform to that standard or guarantee the same level of protection (ibid., para 168). A standard that does not conform will need to have standards based on a risk assessment (*US/Canada-Continued Suspension*, AB, para 532) in line with Articles 5.1 and 5.7. Two scenarios have been determined to be relevant to the application of Article 3.3 in applying a higher level of restriction:

1 If there is scientific justification, that is, a rational relationship between the measure and the available scientific evidence (*Japan-Agricultural Products II*, AB, para 79); or
2 Where a Member determines it to be appropriate in line with Article 5 (*EC-Hormones*, AB, paras 173, 175, and 176).

It is equally important to read subarticle 3.3 in line with the overall objective of the Article which is, broadly, to harmonise national standards whilst allowing Members the right of protection over the life and health of their people, but not the right to impose discriminatory trade restrictive measures that are not for that purpose (*EC-Hormones*, AB, para 177). Members can decided their own (qualified) level of protection (*EC-Hormones*, AB, paras 172–173) and may be reflective of the precautionary principle (ibid., para 124). It does not need to conform to an international standard and can be more stringent (US/Canada-Continued Suspension, AB, para 532) based on scientific evidence or on application of Article 5 (*EC-Hormones*, AB, paras 173, 175, and 176).

Current scientific standards reflecting best practice are the most relevant for basing a measure (*India-Agricultural Products*, PR, paras 7.209–7.210). However, parties cannot be expected to know the latest science if claims and defenses were filed before the new standard was known because the primary legal right of defending oneself cannot be impinged (*India-Agricultural Products*, PR, para 7.211; *Russia-Pigs (EU)*, PR, para 7.265). Latest science takes time to be incorporated into international codes. Therefore, the delay period between science to incorporation into international standards and then the further inability to Members to justify late changes based on those measures without violation, is crucially problematic for those areas where even a minor incursion of bacteria or virus may have devastating consequences. In the case where Members find even the international standards incorrect for certain diseases, reliance must be had on subarticles 3.2 and 3.3.

3.7.3 The issue of delay

Denoting a reasonable delay is a question of what justifiable and works to ensure market access for the exporter, focusing on timeliness of the importer. Justifiable delay caused by a failure of the exporter to failure to answer/provide information required by the importer, is justifiable.[39]

In *EC-Approval and Marketing of Biotech Products*, "delay" was noted to be "a period of time lost by inaction or inability to proceed" and noted that OIE guidelines and the US Animal and Plant Health Inspection Service (APHIS) standard processing times serve as important indicators of a reasonable length of time (para 7.117).[40] The US APHIS standards for timeliness were assessed in the *US-animals* dispute and comparison with other assessments was used: "the Panel assessed whether a period of more than one and a half years was reasonable. The Panel noted that it took APHIS only between four and 13 months to assess whether to permit imports from Uruguay, Santa Catarina (a state in Southern Brazil), and Japan, and concluded that a period of over one year was "neither ordinary nor expected" (para 7.154). The Panel faulted the United States for a process that falls outside of the "ordinary" while recognising that APHIS does not have a clearly articulated timeline by which to judge its determination.[41]

3.7.4 Regional versus international standards

International standard-setting bodies also discount application of standards of regional or inter-regional organisations, so Arctic/ Antarctic organisations which may have the necessary knowledge either will not be relevant to standard-setting or else the measures they seek to implement will be subject to delay as the international organisations deliberate over their implementation (Gruszczynski 2010,

80).[42] SPS standard-setting is subject to voting protocols which may suffer from ulterior motives and need formal approval (Gruszczynski 2010, 87 and 89).

3.8 TBT Agreement

Technical regulations under the Agreement on Technical Barriers to Trade (TBT Agreement)[43] have a rebuttable presumption that they are not obstacles to trade where they are in accordance with international standards as per Article 2.5 (*EC-Sardines*, AB, para 214).[44] International standards do not require consensus to be used in this regard (ibid., para 222–227).

The link between the SPS Agreement and the TBT Agreement is in the harmonisation standards set out in Article 3 SPS in relation to the idea of "based on". Similarly to Article 3.1 SPS, "based" on does not mean conformity with but rather used as a basis for (*EC-Hormones*, AB, para 166; PR, para 7.110; reiterated in *EC-Sardines*, AB, paras 242 and 244).

Principles of non-discrimination and reasonable time apply, though arguably a reasonable time may fall fowl of preventing transmissibility of disease (in particular, see Article 2.12):

> 2.12 Except in those urgent circumstances referred to in paragraph 10, Members shall allow a reasonable interval between the publication of technical regulations and their entry into force in order to allow time for producers in exporting Members, and particularly in developing country Members, to adapt their products or methods of production to the requirements of the importing Member.

The crux of Article 3 SPS is in its persuasive (more than obligating) role in bringing Members' provisions into alignment. Article 2.4 TBT Agreement also refers to the notion of "based on" being one of non-contradiction. However, there is a question as to whether the TBT applies in the case of the SPS Agreement; Article 1.5 TBT states specifically, "The provisions of this Agreement do not apply to sanitary and phytosanitary measures as defined in Annex A of the Agreement on the Application of Sanitary and Phytosanitary Measures". As the SPS shares the bilateral nature of international trade rules, the scope for applicability of TBT measure where SPS measures are not put in place (either because they are not recognised to be necessary or because the science lags the trade preference) is wide. Where the TBT does apply, preference is, as with all WTO law, given to non-discriminatory trade practices. Article 2.2 states:

"Members shall ensure that technical regulations are not prepared, adopted or applied with a view to or with the effect of creating unnecessary obstacles to international trade...technical regulations shall not be more trade-restrictive than necessary to fulfil a legitimate objective...[such as] national security requirements; the prevention of deceptive practices; *protection of human health or safety, animal or plant life or health, or the environment.* In assessing such risks, relevant elements of consideration are, inter alia: available scientific and technical information, related processing technology or intended end-uses of products". (emphasis added)

Assessments ensure like-treatment and application of standards of conformity (Article 5) "in cases where a positive assurance of conformity with technical regulations or standards is required" (Article 5.1) applying like treatment (5.2.1). Conformity assessment procedures are outlined in Articles 5.1 and 5.2, and conformity assurances relaxed where, even though international standards exist or are soon to exist, it is inappropriate on the basis of *"protection of human health or safety, animal or plant life or health, or the environment; fundamental climatic or other geographical factors"* (Article 5.4). Where international standards do not exist, the notification and non-discriminatory provisions required when a Member proposes to introduce a conformity assessment procedure do not in their entirety need to be considered where "urgent problems of safety, health, environmental protection or national security arise or threaten to arise for a Member" (Article 5.7) provided notification of the nature of the urgent problem is indicated to the Secretariat (Article 5.7.1). Where a positive assurance is required, international systems are to be adhered to (Article 9.1), with Members taking reasonable measures to ensure these "international and regional systems ... comply with the provisions of Articles 5 and 6" (Article 9.2).

3.9 PSI Agreement

Under the Agreement on Preshipment Inspection (PSI Agreement),[45] the same standards of transparency and non-discrimination apply. The major strength of the PSI Agreement is the method of appointing the panel: with one member appointed by the PSI entities, one from an entity representing exporters and one independent member who appears to hold the balance of power under Article 4. This leaves an element of independence in resolving disputes between exporters and inspection agencies, though whether the latter absolutely have the importer-nation's interest in mind is another question.

Problematic with the PSI Agreement is that, as with the provisions of WTO agreements, the nature is primarily bilateral in nature (Gruszczynski 2010, 172). Agreements are between buyer and seller, leaving open the possibility of unequal bargaining power:

> User Members shall ensure that quantity and quality inspections are performed in accordance with the standards defined by the seller and the buyer in the purchase agreement and that, in the absence of such standards, relevant international standards apply. (PSI, Article 4)

In addition, the confidential privilege given to Member export-import arrangements (PSI, Article 9) may encourage a lack of transparency because under Article 10, Members are not required to disclose confidential information which would "jeopardize the effectiveness of the preshipment inspection programmes or would prejudice the legitimate commercial interest of particular enterprises, public or private". In emergency situations (addressed by Articles XX and XXI of GATT 1994), pre-shipment inspection can apply additional requirements prior to informing an exporter: "[h]owever, in emergency situations of the types, such additional requirements or changes may be applied to a shipment before the exporter has been informed. This assistance shall not, however, relieve exporters from their obligations in respect of compliance with the import regulations of the user Members" (PSI, Article 2 (6)).

3.10 Article 4: The problem with equivalence

Equivalence

1 Members shall accept the sanitary or phytosanitary measures of other Members as equivalent, even if these measures differ from their own or from those used by other Members trading in the same product, if the exporting Member objectively demonstrates to the importing Member that its measures achieve the importing Member's appropriate level of sanitary or phytosanitary protection. For this purpose, reasonable access shall be given, upon request, to the importing Member for inspection, testing and other relevant procedures.

2 Members shall, upon request, enter into consultations with the aim of achieving bilateral and multilateral agreements on recognition of the equivalence of specified sanitary or phytosanitary measures.

Conversely to Article 2.1 which entitles trade restrictions on the basis of prevailing animal, plant, and human life and health, which may support a region of endemism, the equivalence provision undermines it. In this sense, the recognition of Arctic zones as distinct, even within country borders may be necessary to enable fair trade between Arctic areas and also trade restrictions from lower latitudes. Endemic regions evolve, they may not always be disease-free. The movement of pathogens and new susceptibilities of flora and fauna make unknown qualitative and quantitative damage which will occur if we allow free trade to take precedence over unknown disease-host-environment interactions. Thus, the problem with disease-free status and the requirements for specifying continued disease-free status which requires human intrusion, and consequently possible incursion. There is no global equivalence in terms of biodiversity nor in terms of ecosystem resilience, yet equivalence of trade is mandated under Article 4. It may be acknowledged that the Arctic and Antarctic have markedly different faunal species than other places on the planet and from each other, and so the use of Article 4 is restricted, its application concerning trade in the same product.

Knowing with certainty the prevalence of pathogens within the polar regions, likely transmission routes of new and emerging pathogens or, crucially, the susceptibility of endemic animals and their products to such new and emerging pathogens (important where other exportation/importation standards are based on the *prevalence* of a particular pathogen and not its absolute absence, that is, reduced risk not risk-free), is unlikely. Consequently it is equally unlikely that Members on the polar brim will be able to either demonstrate objectively that SPS levels have been reached to the satisfaction of an importer or, where it is the polar region which is the importer, that any testing/inspection done by an exporter would be beneficial, given as the conditions for testing are unmatched to the polar region.

The obligation to determine the ALOP under Article 4.1 (Appellate Body Report, *Australia-Salmon*, para 205) along with Article 4 is to be generally read in conjunction with other provisions of the SPS Agreement, including that technical information supporting an exporter's SPS measure needs to be analysed with reference to the stated ALOP (*US-Poultry (China)*, PR, paras 7.136–7.137). Thus far, the case law has not further clarified the Article. A document, made in 2001 by the SPS Committee, called the Decision on the Implementation of Article 4, stated that the provision may relate to specific measures, certain products or entire systems (10 G/SPS/19/

Rev.2). Further specifics were outlined regarding the procedure to be followed for assessing equivalence and include the following:

- An explanation by the importing Member of the objective or rationale for the SPS measure, including the ALOP;
- Requests from an exporting Member should be replied to within six months and an assessment for equivalence by an importing Member should consider the science-based and technical information provided by the exporting Member to compare the relevant SPS measures;
- The exporting Member shall provide science-based and technical information to support its objective demonstration of the importer's ALOP and the importing Member may request access for inspection, testing and other procedures associated with the equivalence assessment;
- Historical trade in products should be taken into consideration (which may be problematic and irrelevant where fundamental climatic shift alters the resilience and eco-dynamic of the importer's territory);
- The duty not to interrupt or suspend imports, regardless of a request by an exporting Member (which appears to place the onus of proving a necessary interruption on the importing Member); however, if an exporter identifies a product which may be an issue, perhaps disruption to trade on this product ought to be based on the necessary identification. An importing Member may still put in place measures to achieve its ALOP;
- An approach for establishing an objective basis for comparison of equivalent SPS measures may consider the Codex or OIE approach;
- Technical assistance, especially for developing countries to facilitate implementation of Article 4, should be considered;
- The Codex Alimentarius Commission, the World Organisation for Animal Health and the Interim Commission on Phytosanitary Measures are tasked with developing guidelines on equivalence of SPS measures and to remain in contact with the Committee (G/SPS/19/Rev.2, paras 9 and 10).

It is difficult to determine, at the present time, what impact Article 4 might have on the polar regions: whether it might be a further hindrance to protective and precautionary measures or a bolster to them.

Notes

1. The Agreement on the Application of Sanitary and Phytosanitary Measures (the "SPS Agreement") entered into force with the establishment of the World Trade Organisation on 1 January 1995, World Trade Organisation < https://www.wto.org/english/tratop_e/sps_e/spsagr_e.htm> accessed 8 March 2018.
2. Australia—Measures Affecting the Importation of Apples from New Zealand, WT/DS367/AB/R 29 November 2010.
3. Lim, J. H., 2011. Liver flukes: The malady neglected. Korean Journal of Radiology, 12(3), 269–279. https://doi.org/10.3348/kjr.2011.12.3.269.
4. International partnership to address human-animal-environment health risks gets a boost, WHO, https://www.who.int/zoonoses/Tripartite-partnership/en/ 3 July 2020.
5. India—Measures Concerning the Importation of Certain Agricultural Products, WT/DS430/AB/R 4 June 2015.
6. Silverglade, B.A., 2000. The WTO Agreement on Sanitary and Phytosanitary Measures: Weakening Food Safety Regulations to Facilitate Trade? Food Drug Law Journal. 55(4):517–524, 6.
7. Ibid.
8. Russian Federation—Measures on the Importation of Live Pigs, Pork and Other Pig Products from the European Union WT/DS475/24 23 February 2017.
9. India—Measures Concerning the Importation of Certain Agricultural Products, WT/DS430/41. https://www.wto.org/english/tratop_e/dispu_e/cases_e/ds430_e.htm.
10. See for example, Power, M.L,, Samuel, A., Smith, J.J., Starke, J.S., Gillings, M.R., Gordon, D.M. 2016. *Escherichia coli* out in the cold: Dissemination of human-derived bacteria into the Antarctic microbiome. Environmental Pollution. 215, 58–65.
11. Kevin C. Kennedy, 2000. "Resolving International Sanitary and Phytosanitary Disputes in the WTO: Lessons and Future Directions", Food & Drug Law Journal. 55, 81.
12. United States—Certain Measures Affecting Imports of Poultry from China WT/DS392/5 5 November 2010.
13. Prescott, J., Feldmann, H., Safronetz, D., 2017. Amending Koch's postulates for viral disease: When "growth in pure culture" leads to a loss of virulence. Antiviral Research, 137, 1–5. https://doi.org/10.1016/j.antiviral.2016.11.002; Koch R. 1884. Die Aettiologie der Tuberkulose; pp. 1–88. Mitt Kaiser Gesundh.
14. European Communities—Measures Concerning Meat and Meat Products (Hormones), WT/DS26/29 17 April 2014.
15. Japan—Measures Affecting the Importation of Apples, WT/DS245/AB/R 26 November 2003.
16. Japan—Measures Affecting the Importation of Apples, WT/DS245/R 15 July 2003.
17. Russian Federation—Measures on the Importation of Live Pigs, Pork and Other Pig Products from the European Union, WT/DS475/R 19 August 2016.
18. The footnote to Article 3.3 defines "scientific justification" as an "examination and evaluation of available scientific information in conformity with relevant provisions of this Agreement ..."

19. Australia—Measures Affecting Importation of Salmon. WT/DS18 (1998).
20. Costa Rica—Measures Concerning the Importation of Fresh Avocados from Mexico - Request for the establishment of a panel by Mexico, WT/DS524/2.
21. Costa Rica—Measures Concerning the Importation of Fresh Avocados from Mexico 8 March 2017. Found at < https://docs.wto.org/dol2fe/Pages/FE_Search/FE_S_S009-DP.aspx?language=E&Catalogue-IdList=235023&CurrentCatalogueIdIndex=0&FullTextHash=&HasEnglishRecord=True&HasFrenchRecord=True&HasSpanishRecord=True> accessed 8 September 2017.
22. Costa Rica—Measures Concerning the Importation of Fresh Avocados from Mexico—Request for Consultations by Mexico, WT/DS524/1.
23. Costa Rica—Measures Concerning the Importation of Fresh Avocados from Mexico—Request for the Establishment of a Panel by Mexico, WT/DS524/2.
24. Griffin, History of the Development of the SPS Agreement, Module 1 in III. Agreement on the Application of Sanitary and Phytosanitary Measures (SPS) and Agreement on Technical Barriers to Trade (TBT), http://www.fao.org/3/x7354e/X7354e01.htm accessed 10.08.2019.
25. Gruszczynski, L., 2010. Regulating Health and Environmental Risks under WTO Law: A Critical Analysis of the SPS Agreement, Oxford Online, 80.
26. This is contrary to the argument put forward by Gruszczynski with regard to a presumption of consistency for Article 2.4: "This approach, however, does not find sufficient support in the language of the SPS Agreement and also seems to be incompatible with the cumulative nature of the obligations provided by GATT 1994 and the SPS Agreements" (Gruszczynski, 94).
27. Japan—Measures Affecting Agricultural Products, WT/DS76/AB/R 22 February 1999.
28. Japan — Measures Affecting the Importation of Apples, WT/DS245/AB/R 26 November 2003.
29. Canada—Continued Suspension of Obligations in the EC-Hormones Dispute, WT/DS321/AB/R 16 October 2008.
30. European Communities—Measures Concerning Meat and Meat Products (Hormones), WT/DS48/R/CAN 18 August 1997.
31. European Communities—Measures Concerning Meat and Meat Products (Hormones), WT/DS26/R/USA 18 August 1997.
32. United States—Certain Measures Affecting Imports of Poultry from China, WT/DS392/R 29 September 2010.
33. Australia—Measures Affecting the Importation of Apples from New Zealand, WT/DS367/R 9 August 2010.
34. European Communities—Measures Affecting the Approval and Marketing of Biotech Products, WT/DS291/R 29 September 2006.
35. Citing Rio Declaration on Environments and Development, UN A/Conf 151/5/Rev 1 14 June 1992.
36. United States—Measures Affecting the Importation of Animals, Meat and Other Animal Products from Argentina, WT/DS447/R 24 July 2015.
37. WTO, "Technical Barriers to Trade" https://www.wto.org/english/tratop_e/tbt_e/tbt.htm 13 July 2020.

38. India—Measures Concerning the Importation of Certain Agricultural Products, WT/DS430/AB/R 4 June 2015.
39. Bown, Chad P., Hillman, Jennifer A., 2017. Foot-and-Mouth Disease and Argentina's Beef Exports: The WTO's US–Animals Dispute. Published online by Cambridge University Press: 10 March 2017. DOI: https://doi.org/10.1017/S1474745616000537.
40. Ibid.
41. Ibid., part 3.1
42. Gruszczynski, L., 2010. Regulating Health and Environmental Risks under WTO Law: A Critical Analysis of the SPS Agreement, Oxford Online, 80.
43. Agreement on Technical Barriers to Trade, TBT, 1868 U.N.T.S. 120.
44. European Communities—Trade Description of Sardines, WT/DS231/AB/R 26 September 2002.
45. Agreement on Preshipment Inspection, 1868. U.N.T.S. 368.

Suggested readings

Agreement on Preshipment Inspection,1868. UNTS 368.

Agreement on Technical Barriers to Trade, TBT, 1868. UNTS 120.

Australia—Measures Affecting Importation of Salmon, WT/DS18 1998.

Australia—Measures Affecting the Importation of Apples from New Zealand, WT/DS367/AB/R 29 November 2010.

Australia—Measures Affecting the Importation of Apples from New Zealand, WT/DS367/R 9 August 2010.

Canada—Continued Suspension of Obligations in the EC-Hormones Dispute, WT/DS321/AB/R 16 October 2008.

Chad P., B., Jennifer A., H. 2017. Foot-and-Mouth Disease and Argentina's Beef Exports: The WTO's US–Animals Dispute. Published online by Cambridge University Press: 10 March 2017. doi: https://doi.org/10.1017/S1474745616000537.

Costa Rica—Measures Concerning the Importation of Fresh Avocados from Mexico—Request for Consultations by Mexico, WT/DS524/1 3 March 2017.

Costa Rica—Measures Concerning the Importation of Fresh Avocados from Mexico—Request for the Establishment of a Panel by Mexico, WT/DS524/2 27 November 2018.

European Communities—Measures Affecting the Approval and Marketing of Biotech Products, WT/DS291/R 29 September 2006.

European Communities—Measures Concerning Meat and Meat Products (Hormones), WT/DS26/29 17 April 2014.

European Communities—Measures Concerning Meat and Meat Products (Hormones), WT/DS48/R/CAN 18 August 1997.

European Communities—Measures Concerning Meat and Meat Products (Hormones), WT/DS26/R/USA 18 August 1997.

European Communities—Trade Description of Sardines, WT/DS231/AB/R 26 September 2002.

Griffin, History of the Development of the SPS Agreement, Module 1 in III. Agreement on the Application of Sanitary and Phytosanitary Measures (SPS) and Agreement on Technical Barriers to Trade (TBT), http://www.fao. org/3/x7354e/X7354e01.htm accessed 10.08.2019.

Gruszczynski, L., 2010. Regulating Health and Environmental Risks under WTO Law: A Critical Analysis of the SPS Agreement, Oxford Online, 80.

India—Measures Concerning the Importation of Certain Agricultural Products, WT/DS430/R 14 October 2014.

India—Measures Concerning the Importation of Certain Agricultural Products, WT/DS430/41. https://www.wto.org/english/tratop_e/dispu_e/cases_e/ds430_e.htm.

International partnership to address human-animal-environment health risks gets a boost, WHO, https://www.who.int/zoonoses/Tripartite-partnership/en/ 3 July 2020.

Japan—Measures Affecting Agricultural Products, WT/DS76/AB/R 22 February 1999.

Japan—Measures Affecting the Importation of Apples, WT/DS245/AB/R 26 November 2003.

Japan—Measures Affecting the Importation of Apples, WT/DS245/R 15 July 2003.

Kennedy, K.C., 2000. "Resolving international sanitary and phytosanitary disputes in the WTO: Lessons and future directions", Food & Drug Law Journal 55, 81.

Lim, J.H. (2011). Liver flukes: The malady neglected. Korean Journal of radiology. 12(3), 269–279. https://doi.org/10.3348/kjr.2011.12.3.269.

Prescott, J., Feldmann, H., Safronetz, D. 2017. Amending Koch's postulates for viral disease: When "growth in pure culture" leads to a loss of virulence. Antiviral Research, 137, 1–5. https://doi.org/10.1016/j.antiviral.2016.11.002; Koch R. 1884. Die Aettiologie der Tuberkulose; pp. 1–88. Mitt Kaiser Gesundh.

Power, M.L., Samuel, A., Smith, J.J., Starke, J.S., Gillings, M.R., Gordon, D.M. 2016. Escherichia coli out in the cold: Dissemination of human-derived bacteria into the Antarctic microbiome. Environmental Pollution. 215, 58–65.

Regulating Health and Environmental Risks under WTO Law: A Critical Analysis of the SPS Agreement, Lukasz Gruszczynski, Oxford Online, 2010, 80.

Rio Declaration on Environments and Development, UN A/Conf 151/5/Rev 1 14 June 1992.

Russian Federation—Measures on the Importation of Live Pigs, Pork and Other Pig Products from the European Union WT/DS475/24 23 February 2017.

Russian Federation—Measures on the Importation of Live Pigs, Pork and Other Pig Products from the European Union, WT/DS475/R 19 August 2016.

Silverglade, B.A. 2000. The WTO agreement on sanitary and phytosanitary measures: Weakening food safety regulations to facilitate trade? Food and Drug Law Journal. 55(4), 517–524.

The Agreement on the Application of Sanitary and Phytosanitary Measures (the "SPS Agreement") entered into force with the establishment of the World Trade Organization on 1 January 1995, World Trade Organization < https:// www.wto.org/english/tratop_e/sps_e/spsagr_e.htm> accessed 8 March 2018.

United States—Certain Measures Affecting Imports of Poultry from China WT/DS392/5 5 November 2010.

United States—Certain Measures Affecting Imports of Poultry from China WT/DS392/R 29 September 2010.

United States—Measures Affecting the Importation of Animals, Meat and Other Animal Products from Argentina WT/DS447/R 24 July 2015.

WTO, "Technical Barriers to Trade" https://www.wto.org/english/tratop_e/tbt_e/tbt_e.htm 13 July 2020.

4 Cooperation and governance

GLOBAL HEALTH STRATEGY

On 8 March 2017, a request for consultation was filed with the DSU for alleged violations of Article 11.1[1] of the *WTO Agreement on the Application of Sanitary and Phytosanitary Measures* (SPS Agreement)[2]: an alleged violation of a measure to prevent the importation of a product that might threaten the health status of plant, animal, or human health. Basic entitlements under the SPS Agreement include the ability to "take sanitary and phytosanitary measures necessary for the protection of human, animal, or plant life or health" (Article 2.1). Such measures are critical for the contamination of disease and pathogen spread through the movement of products across borders. Surveillance to detect trade sanctions violations[3] may serve a role of keeping nations on a path to conciliatory trade relations, even though it entails sacrifice of the underlying traits of sovereign entitlement.

In this concluding chapter, the problems of international cooperation are mentioned as the major impediment to successful monitoring of trade in disease. Given the competing claims over territorial control in Antarctica (in the sense of both acknowledged and overlapping and not acknowledged claims)[4] and the various interests of the littoral states of the Arctic, the future of cooperation has one large opponent: national interests.[5] In the Arctic, the Arctic Council may play an increased role in resolving differences between Arctic States[6] which may place the Arctic in a slightly more promising position than the Antarctic where the future of the Antarctic Treaty System (ATS) and associated agreements rests on precarious grounds.[7]

This chapter is included as a way of introducing jurisdictional issues which may be relevant for further research in so far as they may hinder the development of control of and surveillance of pathogeneses. It is unknown presently as the collaborative mechanisms for surveillance are only now being implemented[8] and surveillance itself presents several conflicting desires such as privacy or greater transparency. With climate shift,[9] border control and strict quarantine measures will rise, giving rise to market barriers and impediments to local trade. Whilst this may provide a hindrance to pathogenic transfer, border quarantine at land-borders does not necessarily prevent the passage of animals, birds, or water and the transfer of pathogens.

4.1 Global health governance, infectious disease and sovereignty: Cooperation problems

The necessity to deliver a global health strategy, one that focuses on the science and the sharing of disease information, has had several well-marked way markers. Not simply the outbreak of Ebola in the Democratic Republic of the Congo,[10] nor the SARS epidemic,[11] not even MERS in the Middle-East,[12] but the rise of various contagions among animal populations, including distemper virus, avulavirus (which has been found to be ubiquitous in the studied penguin populations in Antarctica) and even zoonotic infections in husbanded equines.[13] Further to this is evidence of a disparate approach to sharing information; one example is the case of Indonesia withholding samples of H5N1 virus from international scientific research, citing sovereign rights.[14]

It is a possibility that nations, in particular those with national sovereignty over parts of the Arctic, may withhold (or be withholding) scientific data on disease and its transmission, that is, whether what is reported in the scientific literature is just part of what is occurring. In other parts of the world, where disease burdens are highest, there remains a lack of location-based research and reporting inclusion,[15] something which a focus on the inclusion of local partners[16] and local funders at the initial stages of global collaborative networks on disease and trade may curb.

In the 2020 update for the polar programs written by the Congressional Research Service of the United States, the first three goals of the National Science Foundation's (NSF) Navigating the New Arctic Plan include aims which involve scientific research and may be broad enough to include disease and trade, but does not specifically state this:

"1 Improved understanding of Arctic change and its local and global effects that capitalizes on: innovative and optimized observation infrastructure; advances in understanding of fundamental processes; and new approaches to modelling (sic) interactions among the natural environment, built environment, and social systems.

2 New and enhanced research communities that are diverse, integrative, and well-positioned to carry out productive research on the interactions or connections between Arctic natural and built environments and social systems and how these connections inform our understanding of Arctic change and its local and global effects.
3 Research outcomes that inform U.S. national security, economic development, and societal well-being and enable resilient, sustainable Arctic communities".[17]

The absence of trade and disease mentioned specifically is an omission from the agenda, as the importance of One Health[18] is key to ensuring the persistence of "resilient, sustainable Arctic communities", including people and animals.

4.2 Who's Responsible? The issue of jurisdiction

4.2.1 *Governance of the Arctic: Does the SPS have a role?*

Whether the littoral countries of the Arctic, or those which have current claims over the Antarctic are Members of the SPS Agreement is the first possible restriction to its operation, especially given the Agreement relies on Members' implementation of harmonised standards to operate. The second restriction is over those areas not under a particular Members' jurisdiction. In so far as the Arctic has an area of high seas not under the sole jurisdiction of a Member,[19] the application of the SPS Agreement controlling the flow of tradable products may not be applicable.

One area where jurisdictional challenges play an important role is in Arctic fisheries development and management. Whether the ethics of increasing commercial fishing in Arctic waters are agreeable, their presence introduces challenges of introduced disease and altered eco-dynamics by the presence of large numbers of fish in one area (which change the turbidity, faecal content and temperature of the surrounding waters) and, as the water warms and the faunal barriers shift, as will the species composition, with the introduction of species hitherto alien to the area. Action for developing science in this domain ought to fall to the Arctic Council, as argued by Christiansen et al. (2014):

"an ambitious interdisciplinary science plan across social and natural sciences, and involving Arctic residents, should be outlined and implemented as a precautionary and fundamental measure to meet large-scale human intervention in understudied Arctic waters…"

Uncoordinated efforts and failure to involve educational institutions frustrates these objectives; argues giving the Arctic Council oversight would better coordinate these endeavours.[20] Arctic bodies responsible for maintaining sanitary trade standards can utilise the SPS Agreement as the Arctic itself is, for the most part, clearly jurisdictionally delineated. Where the SPS Agreement is understood to apply as a bilateral tool regulating market access and trade, the application is ensured. This is not the same for Antarctica.

4.2.2 Governance of the Antarctic: Can the SPS have a role?

Issues of jurisdiction in Antarctica are well discussed,[21] yet with no mandated Council and no executive body, the question of responsibility remains outstanding. Under the ATS, conservation is through the Convention on the Conservation of Antarctic Marine Living Resources (CCAMLR),[22] policy and scientific decisions and interchange of information are by and through the Consultative Meetings (ATCM),[23] and facilitation by the Executive Secretary seems to evade the designation of responsibility for protection, focusing rather on facilitation. Disease is a major threat to the Antarctic ecosystem, much the same as in the high North, with temperature changes and ice disturbance leading to increased transmission opportunities. The most apt document to cover risk assessments for the transmission of disease is the one that already exists with an article reserved for endemic environments: the SPS Agreement and its Article 6.

Most problematic, and the largest oversight, is the very *nature* of the SPS Agreement and the possibility that its application to a multilateral treaty system itself may not be legitimate. As already discussed, the SPS Agreement forms part of the WTO Accords, which are bilateral in their nature of application. The application of the SPS risk assessment strategy to Antarctica where there is no national jurisdiction to make bilateral accords,[24] gives rise to the question whether the SPS Agreement can *de jure* or *de facto* be applied to Antarctica.

4.3 Surveillance systems for protection against pathogen importation in the Arctic and Antarctic

Inter-arctic coordination efforts to enhance effective control of infectious diseases gained their own surveillance network for human health through the International Circumpolar Surveillance program of invasive bacterial diseases: a network of hospitals, laboratories, and other agencies to share information on the epidemiology of infectious disease across the Arctic.[25] Such a network of interested public health persons and bodies across the Arctic would be even more effective if it were to incorporate the animal-ecosystem-human interface, making a holistic "one health" approach, more accurately including source, carrier, and naïve populations of infectious and zoonotic disease and potential impacts on food security.[26] Health collaboration and surveillance along with the involvement of One Health has been a major theme of the Arctic Network since 2010.[27] Given the rapid spread of and increasing probability of epidemics, the surveillance of the poles will be significant.

Monitoring disease outbreak in real-time will also prove useful for disease tracking and zoning, and crucial, therefore, for advancing and administering changes in food security trade measures and higher levels of protection. Surveillance may track geomorphological changes that could lead to an ecotoxicological or epidemiological event, and data aggregation and dissemination to national contact points could aid rapid and widespread intergovernmental prevention and control strategies. [28]

Delineated on the basis of geographic distinction (that is, a mountain forms a natural barrier), disease zoning can perhaps be better managed and implemented with the use of better surveillance.[29] Disease zoning brings about environmental protection and the minimisation of contagion, vital where the prevalence of disease epizootics is a new threat to human populations, our food sources, and also to the environment.[30] Disease mapping applies to observation of crops and animals; mapping of disease clusters; making predictions for vulnerable populations; conservation efforts; and agrometeorological and hydrological tele-medicine[31] made all the more valuable when in real-time, adding efficiency to the work of local, regional, and global health organisations. Council of Managers of National Antarctic Programs (COMNAP)[32] could be an organisation which could take on the function of surveillance, being responsible for bringing together 30 National Antarctic Programs and facilitating partnerships and expeditions on the Southern continent. With a long history of scientific research, coordination, and operational involvement, it may be a wise choice.[33] However, a newly devised organisation, with disease, surveillance, and monitoring as its prime mandates, rather than facilitating international partnerships and with a function to advise the ATS on this unique issue, may give the due weight needed for this function.

Alternatively, a new polar organisation, responsible for independent assessment, monitoring and advising on disease, health, and trade in the polar regions may be the best conclusion: a body with the mandate to operationalise polar veterinary, epidemiological, pathological, and mapping technical knowledge across harsh, cold, and naïve climates and cross-reference knowledge from one pole to the other.

Regardless of the regional body responsible for centralised assessment, monitoring, and enforcement, the crucial information collection relies on national systems. In the Southern hemisphere, networks such as the Servicio Nacional de Salud Animal (SENASA) in Argentina may incorporate disease tracking and surveillance in Antarctica. In Australia, surveillance and control of foodborne illness involves public health agencies, food safety agencies, laboratories, and local government working together. Which agency or agencies participate in an investigation depends on the size and scope of the outbreak.

OzFoodNet,[34] a member of the Communicable Diseases Network Australia (CDNA),[35] is the national network of foodborne disease epidemiologists and surveillance officers. The network is coordinated nationally by the OzFoodNet Central team within the Australian Government Department of Health. OzFoodNet epidemiologists are located within each state and territory health department. Controlling disease at exit-point is also a standard procedure through the use of Hazard Analysis and Critical Control Point (HACCP) used in food production and distribution settings in Australia[36] and the United States.[37]

In the Northern hemisphere, Canadian, American, Norwegian, and Russian health networks may be utilised to feed information into a regional surveillance network. A major impediment to neat streamlined approaches may come from the plethora of organisations involved at national level. In the United States, for example, the number of organisations involved in food monitoring or disease surveillance is as wide as are the diverse reporting lines. The Centre for Disease Control (CDC) is the major organisation responsible for investigation of outbreaks, reporting and surveillance, but there are a large number of other organisations involved in the national surveillance and reporting effort: FoodNet is a surveillance system designed to determine the burden of foodborne disease; BioSense is a syndromic surveillance system; the Electronic Surveillance System for Early Notification of Community-based Epidemics (ESSENCE); and National Retail Data Monitor (NRDM). These operate concurrently with national level agencies, including the US Animal and Plant Health Inspection Service (APHIS); Food and Drug Administration (FDA); Center for Food Safety and Applied Nutrition (CFSAN); US Department of Agriculture (USDA); and Consumer Complaint Monitoring System (CCMS). There are also animal-specific surveillance networks; National Animal Health Surveillance System (NAHSS); National Animal Health Laboratory

Network (NAHLN) and an enteric disease antibiotic-resistance monitoring network; National Antibiotic Resistance Monitoring System (NARMS). Systems for disease tracking are diverse and use different scientific tools: PulseNet, which tracks diseases through standardised pulsed-field gel electrophoresis (PFGE) protocols examining pathogen-specifics; laboratory data handling networks (eLEXNET, PulseNet, Global Salm-Surv, CaliciNet), and laboratory response networks (Laboratory Response Network (LRN); Food Emergency Response Network (FERN); NAHSS, National Plant Diagnostic Network (NPDN); Environmental Response Laboratory Network (ELRN); Integrated Consortium of Laboratory Networks (ICLN)). Disease reporting and communication systems are also non-uniform such as Epi-X and U.S. NORS (National Outbreak Reporting System). which also carry out outbreak response.[38] The benefit of multifarious tools is to broaden the net of capturing harmful pathogens. The downfall is the possibility for overlapping mandates, too widely diversified funding and so concentration of effort on similar problems, thus missing potential pathogens.

The question is whether the national policies incentivise the recording and reporting of biosecurity threats or breaches to the global community. In the situation where exporters are not incentivised to report outbreaks immediately due to the immediate economic and political costs for doing so, this results in information asymmetries.[39] Such information asymmetries may also apply where the OIE relies on national reports.[40] A suggested solution to this is for importer/exporter members to share costs for inspections, whereas currently only the importer is responsible.[41] This is a necessary first solution in the case of the poles. Particularly the Arctic, where the burden of inspection currently falls to the importer only, and may be significant as the *US-Animals* case showed, and there is an unwillingness of exporters to declare possible outbreaks or to withhold disease-status as in the case of developing export standards, this is a major impediment to use of any provisional safeguard measures.[42] Annex C provides no clarification on this other than placing the burden with the importer which, in order to be effective, would need to use on-site inspection visits.[43] Fines may be issued as recompense, but in a naïve environment, once biosecurity is breached, the exposure has already occurred. This brings to the fore the role of veterinarians, well-trained and globally-minded to reporting outbreaks in alternative non-governmentally-based fora, specifically direct to the OIE. However, where the OIE is still only seen as a first step in verifying disease status and setting standards for the WTO Members, even the international body provides a pseudo-regulatory function.[44] Finally, the need for collaboration is increasingly a given. The inception of the Global Outbreak and Response Network (GOARN) in 2000, by the WHO[45] to focus on and respond to global health emergencies is a collaborative effort. Although One Health does not appear to be part of its initial mandate, and thus, transboundary animal disease pushed to the side, the increasing awareness of understanding the animal-human disease interface may encourage either global networks such as this to incorporate animal disease and surveillance or else for a similar network to be conceived.

Notes

1. World Trade Organisation, Costa Rica—Measures Concerning the Importation of Fresh Avocados from Mexico—Request for consultations by Mexico 8 March 2017, https://docs.wto.org/dol2fe/Pages/FE_Search/FE_S_S009-DP.aspx?language=E&CatalogueIdList=2350 23&CurrentCatalogueIdIndex=0&FullTextHash=&HasEnglishRecord =True&HasFrenchRecord=True&HasSpanishRecord=True accessed 8 September 2017.
2. Agreement on the Application of Sanitary and Phytosanitary Measures, 1867 UNTS 493, WTO Doc LT/UR/A-1A/12 15 April 1994.
3. Deeks, A., 2014. An international legal framework for surveillance. VJIL 55(2), 291 at 314.
4. Foggarty, E., Antarctica: Assessing and Protecting Australia's National Interests, Lowy Institute, August 2011.
5. In relation to the Antarctic, see for example, Haward, Marcus, Rothwell, Donald R., Jabour, Julia, Hall, Robert, Kellow, Aynsley, Kriwoken, Lorne, Lugten, Gail, Hemmings, Alan, 2006. Australia's Antarctic agenda. Australian Journal of International Affairs 60(3), 439–456, doi: 10.1080/10357710600865705; Joyner, Christopher C., 2011. United States foreign policy interests in the Antarctic. The Polar Journal 1(1), 17–35, doi: 10.1080/2154896X.2011.569384; Liu, Nengye, 2019. The rise of China and the Antarctic Treaty System? Australian Journal of Maritime & Ocean Affairs 11(2), 120–131, doi: 10.1080/18366503.2019.1589897. In relation to the Arctic, see for example, Mariia, Kobzeva, 2019. China's Arctic policy: Present and future. The Polar Journal 9(1), 94–112, doi: 10.1080/2154896X.2019.1618558; Knecht, Sebastian, Keil, Kathrin, 2013. Arctic geopolitics revisited: Spatialising governance in the circumpolar North. The Polar Journal 3(1), 178–203, doi: 10.1080/2154896X.2013.783276.
6. Background as Arctic Council role in facilitating: Rottem, Svein Vigeland, 2015. A note on the Arctic Council Agreements . Ocean Development & International Law 46(1), 50–59. Arctic centralised implementation of policy defers to national interests currently: Knecht & Keil op cit.
7. Background to collaboration in Antarctica: Hambro, Edvard, 1974. Some notes on the future of the Antarctic Treaty Collaboration. American Journal of International Law 68(2), 217–226.
8. For example, the WAHIS interface of the OIE.

9. Prowse, Terry D., Wrona, Frederick J., Reist, James D., Gibson, John J., Hobbie, John E., Le´vesque, Lucie M.J., Vincent, Warwick F., 2006. Climate change effects on hydroecology of Arctic freshwater ecosystems. A Journal of the Human Environment 35(7), 347–358.
10. Kalenga, Oly Ilunga, Moeti, Matshidiso, Sparrow, Annie, Nguyen, Vinh-Kim, Lucey, Daniel, Ghebreyesus, Tedros A., 2019. The ongoing ebola epidemic in the Democratic Republic of Congo, 2018–2019. N Engl J Med 381, 373–383, doi: 10.1056/NEJMsr1904253.
11. Hung, L.S., 2003. The SARS epidemic in Hong Kong: What lessons have we learned?. J R Soc Med. 96(8), 374–378, doi:10.1258/jrsm.96.8.374.
12. Memish, Ziad A., Perlman, S., Kerkhove, M., Zumla, A., 2020. Middle East respiratory syndrome. The Lancet, 395(10229), 1063–1077.
13. As discussed in previous chapters.
14. Fidler D.P., 2008. Influenza virus samples, international law, and global health diplomacy. Emerg Infect Dis.14(1), 88–94, doi:10.3201/eid1401.070700.
15. Mbaye R., Gebeyehu R., Hossmann S., Mbarga, N., Bih-Neh, E., Eteki, L., Thelma O., Oyerinde, A., Kiti, G., Mburu, Y., Harberer, J., Siedner, M., Okeke, I., Boum, Y., 2019. Who is telling the story? A systematic review of authorship for infectious disease research conducted in Africa, 1980–2016. BMJ Global Health 4, e001855, http://orcid.org/0000-0002-6823-8539.
16. Nsubuga, Peter, White, Mark E., Thacker, Stephen B., Anderson, Mark A., Blount, Stephen B., Broome, Claire V., Chiller, Tom M., Espitia, Victoria, Imtiaz, Rubina, Sosin, Dan, Stroup, Donna F., Tauxe, Robert V., Vijayaraghavan, Maya, Trostle, Murray, 2006. Public Health Surveillance: A Tool for Targeting and Monitoring Interventions. In: Jamison D.T., Breman J.G., Measham A.R., et al., editors. Disease Control Priorities in Developing Countries. 2nd edition. Washington (DC): The International Bank for Reconstruction and Development / The World Bank; 2006. Chapter 53. Available from: https://www.ncbi.nlm.nih.gov/books/NBK11770/ Co-published by Oxford University Press, New York.
17. Congressional Research Service, Changes in the Arctic: Background and Issues for Congress (May 2020),https://crsreports.congress.gov R41153 found at https://fas.org/sgp/crs/misc/R41153.pdf.
18. Ruscio, Bruce A., Brubaker, Michael, Glasser, Joshua, Hueston, Will, Hennessy, Thomas W., 2015. One Health—A strategy for resilience in a changing Arctic. International Journal of Circumpolar Health, 74(1), doi: 10.3402/ijch.v74.27913.
19. Morris, Kathleen, Hossain, Kamrul, 2016. Legal instruments for marine sanctuary in the high Arctic. Laws 5(2), 20, https://doi.org/10.3390/laws5020020.
20. Issues on Arctic marine biodiversity and conservation are addressed by a plethora of intergovernmental forums and nongovernmental organisations (NGOs) such as the Arctic Council, Census of MarineLife (CoML), ICES, IUCN, Ramsar Convention on Wetlands (RAMSAR) and World Wildlife Fund (WWF). Unfortunately, the assessment work is done often in parallel and seems frustratingly disorganised for the scientists involved. Academic institutions, in charge of training prospective scientists, are also little consulted...”; Christiansen, JØrgen S.,

Mecklenburg Catherine W., Karamuschko, Oleg V., 2014. Arctic marine fishes and their fisheries in light of global change. Global Change Biology 20, 352–359, doi: 10.1111/gcb.12395, at 358.
21. Foggarty, op cit.
22. See "Relationship to the Antarctic Treaty System", CCAMLR, https://www.ccamlr.org/en/organisation/relationship-ats 14 July 2020.
23. "ATCM and Other Meetings", Secretariat of the Antarctic Treaty, https://www.ats.aq/e/atcm.html, 14 July 2020.
24. Claims on Antarctica are "frozen": E. Foggarty op cit.
25. Parkinson, A. J., Bruce, M. G., Zulz, T., 2008. International Circumpolar Surveillance, an Arctic network for the surveillance of infectious diseases. Emerging Infectious Diseases 14(1), 18–24. https://doi.org/10.3201/eid1401.070717.
26. As with the Arctic: Ruscio, Bruce A., Brubaker, Michael, Glasser, Joshua, Hueston, Will, Hennessy, Thomas W., 2015. One Health—A strategy for resilience in a changing Arctic. International Journal of Circumpolar Health 74(1), doi: 10.3402/ijch.v74.27913.
27. For example, see Arctic Health Declaration (2011), https://oaarchive.arctic-council.org/bitstream/handle/11374/1058/ACSAO-DK04_5_1_The_Arctic_Health_Declaration.pdf?sequence=1&isAllowed=y 27 June 2020; Arctic One Health: Strategy for Resiliency—Operationalising One Health in the Arctic Overview, agreed at the Arctic Council SAO plenary meeting (eDocs code: ACSAOUS202) 16–17 March 2016, Fairbanks, Alaska, USA accessed < https://oaarchive.arctic-council.org/bitstream/handle/11374/1727/EDOCS-3254-v1-ACSAOUS202_Fairbanks_2016_6-4a_SDWG_Arctic_One_Health_Overview.pdf?sequence=1&isAllowed=y 27 June 2020.
28. See World Health Organisation, "Emerging Zoonoses" https://www.who.int/zoonoses/emerging_zoonoses/en/ accessed 18 December 2019; Ostfeld, R.S., 2009. Biodiversity loss and the rise of zoonotic pathogens. Clinical Microbiology and Infection 15 (Suppl 1), 40–43, doi: 10.1111/j.1469-0691.2008.02691.x. Bagayoko, C.O., Müller, H., Geissbuhler, A., 2006. Assessment of Internet-based tele-medicine in Africa (the RAFT project). Computerized Medical Imaging and Graphics 30 , 407–416.
29. Ibid. Disease zoning allows for the zoning of parcels of land and/or countries owing to the existence and prevalence of diseases within boundaries Food and Agriculture Organisation, Chapter 8 "Disease Zoning" at ftp://ftp.fao.org/docrep/fao/005/y1238e/y1238e08.pdf accessed 1.09.2017.
30. See World Health Organisation, "Emerging Zoonoses" https://www.who.int/zoonoses/emerging_zoonoses/en/ accessed 18 December 2019; Ostfeld, R.S., 2009. Biodiversity loss and the rise of zoonotic pathogens. Clinical Microbiology and Infection 15 (Suppl 1) 40–43, doi: 10.1111/j.1469-0691.2008.02691.x.
31. Bagayoko, C.O., Müller, H., Geissbuhler, A., 2006. Assessment of Internet-based tele-medicine in Africa (the RAFT project). Computerized Medical Imaging and Graphics 30 407–416.
32. Welcome to the Council of Managers of National Antarctic Programs (COMNAP) website, https://www.comnap.aq/ 14 July 2020.
33. Ibid.

34. The Department of Health, "OzFoodNet: Foodborne disease in Australia Annual reports of the OzFoodNet network", Australian Government, https://www1.health.gov.au/internet/main/publishing.nsf/Content/cda-pubs-annlrpt-ozfnetar.htm 14 July 2020.
35. The Department of Health, "Communicable Diseases Network Australia (CDNA)", Australian Government, https://www1.health.gov.au/internet/main/publishing.nsf/Content/cda-cdna-index.htm 14 July 2020.
36. "Everything you need to know about HACCP", Australian Institute of Food Safety https://www.foodsafety.com.au/blog/everything-you-need-to-know-about-haccp 14 July 2020.
37. "HACCP Principles & Application Guidelines", US Food & Drug Administration. https://www.fda.gov/food/hazard-analysis-critical-control-point-haccp/haccp-principles-application-guidelines 14 July 2020.
38. Institute of Medicine (US) Forum on Microbial Threats. Addressing Foodborne Threats to Health: Policies, Practices, and Global Coordination: Workshop Summary. Washington (DC): National Academies Press (US); 2006. 5, Surveillance of the Food Supply. Available from: https://www.ncbi.nlm.nih.gov/books/NBK57083/. John M. Besser, "Systems to Detect Microbial Contamination of the Food Supply".
39. Brown, Chad P., Hillman, Jennifer A., 2017. Foot-and-Mouth Disease and Argentina's Beef Exports: The WTO's US–Animals Dispute. Published online by Cambridge University Press: 10 March 2017. doi: https://doi.org/10.1017/S1474745616000537, section 2.
40. Ibid., section 3.3.
41. Ibid., section 3.3.
42. Ibid., section 3.2.
43. Ibid., section 3.2.
44. Ibid., section 3.2.
45. GOARN, https://extranet.who.int/goarn/

Suggested readings

Agreement on the Application of Sanitary and Phytosanitary Measures, 1867 UNTS 493, WTO Doc LT/UR/A-1A/12 15 April 1994.

Arctic Health Declaration (2011) https://oaarchive.arctic-council.org/bitstream/handle/11374/1058/ACSAO-DK04_5_1_The_Arctic_Health_Declaration.pdf?sequence=1&isAllowed=y 27 June 2020;

Arctic One Health: Strategy for Resiliency—Operationalizing One Health in the Arctic Overview, agreed at the Arctic Council SAO plenary meeting (eDocs code: ACSAOUS202) 16–17 March 2016, Fairbanks, Alaska, USA accessed < https://oaarchive.arctic-council.org/bitstream/handle/11374/1727/EDOCS-3254-v1-ACSAOUS202_Fairbanks_2016_6-4a_SDWG_Arctic_One_Health_Overview.pdf?sequence=1&isAllowed=y 27 June 2020.

Australian Institute of Food Safety, 'Everything you need to know about HACCP', Australian Institute of Food Safety https://www.foodsafety.com.au/blog/everything-you-need-to-know-about-haccp 14 July 2020.

Bagayoko, C.O., Müller, H., Geissbuhler, A., 2006. "Assessment of internet-based tele-medicine in Africa (the RAFT project). Computerized Medical Imaging and Graphics 30, 407–416.

Besser, J.M.. "Systems to Detect Microbial Contamination of the Food Supply".

Brown, C.P., Hillman, J.A. 2017. Foot-and-Mouth Disease and Argentina's Beef Exports: The WTO's US–Animals Dispute. Published online by Cambridge University Press: 10 March 2017. doi: https://doi.org/10.1017/S1474745616000537, section 2.

CCAMLR, "Relationship to the Antarctic Treaty System", CCAMLR, https://www.ccamlr.org/en/organisation/relationship-ats 14 July 2020.

Christiansen, J.ØrgenS., Mecklenburg, C.W., Karamuschko, O.V., 2014. Arctic marine fishes and their fisheries in light of global change. Global Change Biology 20, 352–359, doi: 10.1111/gcb.12395, at 358.

Congressional Research Service, Changes in the Arctic: Background and Issues for Congress (May 2020),https://crsreports.congress.gov R41153 found at https://fas.org/sgp/crs/misc/R41153.pdf.

Costa Rica—Measures Concerning the Importation of Fresh Avocados from Mexico—Request for consultations by Mexico 8 March 2017, https://docs.wto.org/dol2fe/Pages/FE_Search/FE_S_S009-DP.aspx?language=E&CatalogueIdList=235023&CurrentCatalogueIdIndex=0&FullTextHash=&HasEnglishRecord=True&HasFrenchRecord=True&HasSpanishRecord=True [accessed 8 September 2017]

Deeks, A., An International legal framework for surveillance, VJIL, 55(2), 291 at 314.

Fidler, D.P., 2008. Influenza virus samples, international law, and global health diplomacy. Emerging Infectious Diseases 14(1), 88–94. doi: 10.3201/eid1401.070700.

Foggarty, E., "Antarctica: Assessing and Protecting Australia's National Interests", Lowy Institute, August 2011.

Food and Agriculture Organisation, Chapter 8 "Disease Zoning" at ftp://ftp.fao.org/docrep/fao/005/y1238e/y1238e08.pdf accessed 1 September 2017.

Global Outbreak Alert and Response Network. https://extranet.who.int/goarn/

Hambro, E., 1974. "Some notes on the future of the Antarctic treaty collaboration", American Journal of International Law 68(2), 217–226.

Haward, M., Rothwell, D.R., Jabour, J., Hall, R., Kellow, A., Kriwoken, L., Lugten, G., Hemmings, A. 2006.Australia's Antarctic agenda, Australian Journal of International Affairs, 60(3), 439–456, doi: 10.1080/10357710600865705

Hung, L.S., 2003 The SARS epidemic in Hong Kong: What lessons have we learned?. Journal of the Royal Society of Medicine 96(8), 374–378. doi: 10.1258/jrsm.96.8.374.

Institute of Medicine (US) Forum on Microbial Threats. Addressing Foodborne Threats to Health: Policies, Practices, and Global Coordination: Workshop Summary. Washington (DC): National Academies Press (US); 2006. 5, Surveillance of the Food Supply. Available from: https://www.ncbi.nlm.nih.gov/books/NBK57083/.

Joyner, C.C., 2011. United States foreign policy interests in the Antarctic. The Polar Journal 1(1), 17–35. doi: 10.1080/2154896X.2011.569384;.

Kalenga, O.I., Moeti, M., Sparrow, A., Nguyen, V.-K., Lucey, D., Ghebreyesus, T.A., 2019. "The ongoing ebola epidemic in the Democratic Republic of Congo, 2018–2019", New England Journal of Medicine 381, 373–383, doi: 10.1056/NEJMsr1904253.

Knecht, S., Keil, K., 2013. Arctic geopolitics revisited: Spatialising governance in the circumpolar North, The Polar Journal 3(1), 178–203, doi: 10.1080/2154896X.2013.783276.

Kobzeva, M., 2019. China's Arctic policy: Present and future. The Polar Journal 9(1), 94–112. doi: 10.1080/2154896X.2019.1618558;.

Liu, N., 2019. "The rise of China and the Antarctic treaty system?". Australian Journal of Maritime & Ocean Affairs 11(2), 120–131. doi: 10.1080/18366503.2019.1589897.

Mbaye, R., Gebeyehu, R., Hossmann, S., Mbarga, N., Bih-Neh, E., Eteki, L., Thelma, O., Oyerinde, A., Kiti, G., Mburu, Y., Harberer, J., Siedner, M., Okeke, I., Boum, Y., 2019. Who is telling the story? A systematic review of authorship for infectious disease research conducted in Africa, 1980–2016 BMJ Global Health 4, e001855., http://orcid.org/0000-0002-6823-8539.

Memish, Z.A., Perlman, S., Van Kerkhove, M.D., Zumla, A., 2020. "Middle East respiratory syndrome" The Lancet, 395(10229): 1063–1077.

Morris, K., Hossain, K., 2016. Legal instruments for Marine sanctuary in the High arctic, Laws 5(2), 20, https://doi.org/10.3390/laws5020020.

Nsubuga, P., White, M.E., Thacker, S.B., Anderson, M.A., Blount, S.B., Broome, C.V., Chiller, T.M., Espitia, V., Imtiaz, R., Sosin, D., Stroup, D.F., Tauxe, R.V., Vijayaraghavan, M., Trostle, M., 2006. Public Health Surveillance: A Tool for Targeting and Monitoring Interventions. In: Jamison D.T., Breman J.G., Measham A.R., et al., editors. Disease Control Priorities in Developing Countries. 2nd edition. Washington (DC): The International Bank for Reconstruction and Development/The World Bank. Chapter 53. Available from: https://www.ncbi.nlm.nih.gov/books/NBK11770/Co-published by Oxford University Press, New York.

Ostfeld, R.S., 2009. Biodiversity loss and the rise of zoonotic pathogens, Clinical Microbiology and Infection 15(Suppl 1), 40–3, doi: 10.1111/j.1469-0691.2008.02691.x.

Parkinson, A.J., Bruce, M.G., Zulz, T., 2008. International circumpolar surveillance, an arctic network for the surveillance of infectious diseases. Emerging Infectious Diseases, 14(1), 18–24. https://doi.org/10.3201/eid1401.070717.

Prowse, T.D., Wrona, F.J., Reist, J.D., Gibson, J.J., Hobbie, J.E., Le'vesque, L.M.J., Vincent, W.F., 2006. Climate change effects on hydroecology of arctic Freshwater ecosystems. A Journal of the Human Environment, 35(7), 347–358.

Rottem, S.V., 2015. A note on the arctic council agreements, Ocean Development & International Law 46(1), 50–59.

Ruscio, B.A., Brubaker, M., Glasser, J., Hueston, W., Hennessy, T.W. 2015.One health—A strategy for resilience in A changing arctic, International Journal of Circumpolar Health, 74(1), doi: 10.3402/ijch.v74.27913.

Secretariat of the Antarctic Treaty, "ATCM and Other Meetings", Secretariat of the Antarctic Treaty, https://www.ats.aq/e/atcm.html, 14 July 2020.

The Department of Health, "Communicable Diseases Network Australia (CDNA)", Australian Government, https://www1.health.gov.au/internet/main/publishing.nsf/Content/cda-cdna-index.htm 14 July 2020.

The Department of Health, "OzFoodNet: Foodborne Disease in Australia Annual Reports of the OzFoodNet Network", Australian Government, https://www1.health.gov.au/internet/main/publishing.nsf/Content/cda-pubs-annlrpt-ozfnetar.htm 14 July 2020.

US Food & Drug Administration, "HACCP Principles & Application Guidelines", US Food & Drug Administration. https://www.fda.gov/food/hazard-analysis-critical-control-point-haccp/haccp-principles-application-guidelines 14 July 2020.

Welcome to the Council of Managers of National Antarctic Programs (COMNAP) website, https://www.comnap.aq/ 14 July 2020.

World Health Organisation, "Emerging Zoonoses" https://www.who.int/zoonoses/emerging_zoonoses/en/ accessed 18 December 2019.

Index

For Product Safety Concerns and Information please contact our EU
representative GPSR@taylorandfrancis.com
Taylor & Francis Verlag GmbH, Kaufingerstraße 24, 80331 München, Germany

www.ingramcontent.com/pod-product-compliance
Lightning Source LLC
Chambersburg PA
CBHW061830220326
41599CB00027B/5239